DISCARD

Republic of Denial

REPUBLIC OF
DENIAL

Press, Politics,

and Public Life

Michael Janeway

Yale University Press

New Haven & London

Lyric excerpts of "Can You Use Any Money Today?" by Irving Berlin (page 20) copyright © 1950 by Irving Berlin. Copyright renewed. International copyright secured. All rights reserved. Reprinted by permission.

Portions of the introduction and chapter 4 appeared in different form in "Power and Weakness of the Press," the Freedom Forum *Media Studies Journal,* fall 1991. Portions of chapters 5 and 6 appeared in different form in "The Press and Privacy: Rights and Rules," in *The Morality of the Mass Media,* W. Lawson Taitte, ed. (University of Texas at Dallas, 1993).

Designed by April Leidig-Higgins.
Set in Sabon type by Keystone Typesetting, Inc., Orwigsburg, Pennsylvania.
Printed in the United States of America.

Library of Congress Cataloging-in-Publication Data
Janeway, Michael, 1940–   Republic of denial : press, politics, and public life / Michael Janeway.
p. cm.   Includes bibliographical references and index.
ISBN 0-300-08123-5 (alk. paper)
1. Press and politics — United States.   2. Journalism — Political aspects — United States.   3. United States — Politics and government — 20th century.
PN4888.P6J36 1999   071'.3 — dc21   99-30453

A catalogue record for this book is available from the British Library.

The paper in this book meets the guidelines for permanence and durability of the Committee on Production Guidelines for Book Longevity of the Council on Library Resources.

10 9 8 7 6 5 4 3 2 1

Contents

Introduction: A Story of Our Time

POLITICS IN THE United States today is almost universally disdained for falsity and shrillness. The media in the United States are widely condemned for bad practices and attitudes.

This book argues that no solid understanding of one of those states of affairs can be achieved without an understanding of the other, and of the interactions between the two spheres, political and journalistic. It argues further that no sophisticated grasp of them is possible without consideration of how each has evolved over the past thirty years—and of the context of that evolution in the flow of American social, cultural, economic, and political history through those years.

Begin at a beginning.

I

MORE THAN HALF a century ago, democracy triumphed over fascism, not by arms alone. Stirring oratory and the information technologies of the day that disseminated it were among the dictators' essential tools. But words, ideas, and modern mass media were no less instrumental to the leaders of the democracies in turning back the fascist tide.

Winston Churchill inspired his outnumbered countrymen in the Battle of Britain with a series of brilliantly crafted speeches broadcast far and wide. Franklin Roosevelt, as gifted as Churchill in his mastery of radio, gradually persuaded our isolationist nation to become, in the months before Pearl Harbor, "the great arsenal of democracy."

Advancing and following up the oratory, witnesses to the heroic drama, were journalists. Edward R. Murrow observed that Churchill "mobilized the English language, and sent it into battle," and more, that as to sacrifice, "whether defending or attacking, Mr. Churchill never attempted to conceal the cost"; his speeches inspired those who heard them by means of raw truth-telling about Britain's grim position. At home, Republican newspaper publisher William Allen White summed up FDR's bravura wartime leadership in 1943 with an ironic tribute: "Well, darn your old smiling picture, here it is! . . . We, who hate your gaudy guts, salute you."[1]

And so the era's seemingly self-evident lesson was that the fascist dictatorships overreached and fell to the democracies' politics and culture, as well as to their military and industrial might. As a corollary, propaganda — a core instrument of totalitarianism — yielded to modern democratic communication.

FDR's predecessor, Herbert Hoover, had declined to conduct live press conferences, protesting that "the President of the United States will not stand and be questioned like a chicken thief by men whose names he does not even know." Roosevelt saw that democratic leaders had to learn to be accessible; indeed, that direct communication with the public was an opportunity, not a burden.[2]

In the decades that followed, Churchill's and Roosevelt's heroic mobilization of the means of modern communication passed to the archives, became the stuff of film documentaries and nostalgia. Command of an ever more sophisticated, flexible battery of media became available more widely than to just the elite leaders of the democracies. Modern communication began to move to the streets.

In closed societies, in the Soviet Union and Eastern Europe, in Iran, China, the Philippines, and the military regimes of Latin America, a rising chorus of guerrilla radio, television, fax, video, and Internet traffic multiplied the force of crudely printed *samizdat* leaflets of old. Again and again, as in Communist Romania in 1989, when the Ceauşescu regime lost control of the nation's television system, these forms of communication were crucial first to the success and then the fall of modern tyrannies.

Thus, media and democracy seemed to have become productively intertwined, a modern, open marriage of free access between the information marketplace and the political arena.

YET BY THE last decades of the twentieth century, the quality of modern American politics was the subject of widespread despair. An eminent political scientist, Theodore Lowi, wrote that the republic had become "ungovernable . . . a nightmare of administrative boredom." A younger colleague, Michael J. Sandel, argued, "At home and abroad, events spun out of control, and government seemed helpless to respond." Citing a sterile ideological polarization and a collapse of meaningful public life as reasons "why Americans hate politics," a thoughtful journalist, E. J. Dionne, wrote of "a political void that is increasingly filled by the politics of attack and by issues that seem unimportant or contrived." Added Dionne, "We have less and less to do with each other, meaning that we feel few obligations to each other and are less and less inclined to vindicate each other's rights." And in *The Disuniting of America,* liberal historian Arthur M. Schlesinger, Jr., declared of the narcissistic, retrograde aspects of the cult of "multiculturalism," lately eclipsing American ideals of assimilation and integration: "For two centuries Americans had been confident that life would be better for their children than it was for them. . . . Amid foreboding of national decline, Americans now began to look forward less and backward more. The rising cult of ethnicity was a symptom of decreasing confidence in the American future."[3]

PARALLEL TO, BUT almost always unintegrated with the discussion of American political discontents, another chorus decried the conduct and effects of modern mass communication, variously seductive, alienating, subversive, corrupting, corrupted. There was little quarrel about the more exploitative, entertainment-driven media. But critics found even the media's observant priesthood, journalism, increasingly vice-prone. Journalists, it was said, had become a self-righteous elite, drunk on power, obsessed with scandal, blind to the corrosive cynicism they sowed. Or, journalists had become mindless cogs in a faceless, corporatized communications media system.

The press, charged political scientist Thomas E. Patterson, was "out of order." Another, Larry Sabato, offered what became household words in illustration of how: "It has become a spectacle without equal in modern American politics: the news media, print and broadcast, go after a wounded politician like sharks in a feeding frenzy." The effect, he wrote, is to "cheapen . . . public discourse" and "undermine the very credibility of the news profession." Journalist and scholar Suzanne Garment condemned a "nihilism" whereby "reporters view every established leader or organization chiefly as a locus of possible crime."[4]

Such a cult of suspicion "saps people's confidence in politics and public officials, and it erodes both the standing and the standards of journalism," wrote columnist David Broder of *The Washington Post.* "If the assumption is that nothing is on the level, nothing is what it seems, then citizenship becomes a game for fools and there is no point in trying to stay informed." Journalist James Fallows, editor of *U.S. News & World Report* for a term, agreed: "The institution of journalism is not doing its job well now. It is irresponsible with its power. The damage has spread to the public life Americans all share."[5]

On closer inspection, the news business was seen to have divided into two loosely organized camps. One, anxious about journalism's new pariah-like status, sought ways to heal an alleged breach with the public. The second, holding to course, ridiculed the first as unprofessional.

TROUBLE INDEED in democratic paradise.

What had happened to the American institutionalization of political liberty, model for an envious world?

What had happened to American institutions of journalism, long heralded as guarantor of free expression, as judicious "watchdog" and featured player in modern democratic politics?

II

NOT SO LONG ago the press dealt confidently with a world full of exciting, often shocking news, in words and also pictures.[6] More recently it has become terrified of numbers, and of its own shadow.

The news business would be blind and deaf not to be frightened. The numbers that haunt it are undeniably threatening. Once those numbers connoted an ever rising tide of readership, viewership, and advertising revenue, allowing for cyclical disturbances in the economy — a convergence of journalistic and business goals. Once those numbers leaped forward in pace with the expansion and urbanization of the republic, as a function of its political vibrancy. Given captive audiences and advertisers, given family ownership of newspapers and the custodial style of entrepreneurs like Henry Luce and William Paley in magazines and television, the future of the news business used to take care of itself.

No longer. In recent years the numbers have conjured up the specter of mass defection; or, if you prefer, the liberation of captive audiences and advertisers. A tension, building to a conflict, between business goals and journalistic goals. A future for the press that will not take care of itself.

In response to this challenge, those in overall managerial and corporate charge of the news business have reacted on the whole with poverty of imagination and, more to the point, lack of basic news judgment. Instead of looking for the story behind the news, they have adopted a strategy of self-preoccupation. Faulting themselves, not pausing to consider the stars (or Caesar), the great preponderance of them engage in self-abasement and apology for alleged poor performance as journalists and corporate managers.

The worst sins the news business has committed (so goes the self-flagellation) are *elitism, arrogance,* and *failure to know your readers* (or viewers). For "EXTRA: READ ALL ABOUT IT!" now read, "Forgive us for our sins for we know not what we do. Please tell us what *you'd* like us to do." These confused efforts at atonement have as one notable effect the feeding of the press's most narrowly focused critics: those who blame it for the negativism of modern life, and those whose interest lies in driving the news business to become more single-mindedly profit oriented — if necessary, by abandoning the core business of news.

What these news business executives have not done is to order up the application of basic skills of news gathering and analysis in the matter of their audiences' flight from the news. Historians, political scientists, economists, social psychologists, and sociologists — scholars of transition, process, behavior, and the mind, of society and what drives and ails it — might have offered insight into the murky subject of audience defection. Instead of turning to such thinkers, the men and women who run the news business contract with marketing and media consultants; short-order Mr. and Ms. Fix-Its.

The news business behaves in parallel fashion to shore up advertisers' defections as well as audience erosion. With little if any concern for the risk of sabotaging its assets as a one-stop, community-wide instrument of communication, it rushes as to a huckster's miracle cure to trendy techniques for fragmenting its own products and markets.

Panicked by erosion of their market positions, these news business executives' eyes have been on the moment, and on the one impending — the one where the numbers are up for review. In assessing the situation of journalism and their prospects as practitioners of it, most of them have failed to consider the historical and societal roots of their trouble.

In so doing these captains of an industry, the product of which is news and information, have missed the most significant story of our time.

III

THE STORY THE press largely missed, taken as a whole and a cumulative sequence, is the saga of reversal and loss, of breakdown of structures in this country since the 1960s; of social and cultural fragmentation, of public alienation from politics and government; and of erosion of optimism and belief in progress. It's a story that has a profound, fundamental impact on the press — which helps explain why the press missed it.

It's not the only story of our time, and it need not constitute destiny now. But it's the story that dominated American history and spirit in the last third of the twentieth century. It's the real world components of that story that have taken the bloom off the liberations, hopes, and turns for the better of the era. It's the story (together with the facts composing it) that feeds on itself. It's not the only story of our time. But consider it for its power and also its taboo.

In linear terms, the story is about the accumulation in the compressed space of a generation-plus of a series of devastating shocks to the American polity, society, and economy. Even given the collapse of the Soviet Union and the end of the Cold War, even in the sunlight of the economic boom of the 1990s, the long-term effect of those shocks on millions of average citizens was to seem to render them relatively powerless, and the news largely irrelevant. Writ large, the story is about the sobering awakening from the postwar American dream. Of the fading of American command of its own destiny and of the free world's. Of proliferating problems that do not yield to solutions at home, and of loss of command abroad. Of the disintegration of a culture of assurance and consensus, one that embraced near universal concepts of sacrifice and duty — including military service, wartime rationing, broad-based sense of participation in the course of national destiny — into a culture of separatism, self-preoccupied materialism, and doubt. Of the transition from a textured, broadly connected political party system to a rootless swamp of political chicanery and facade. Of the journey of the American economy from seemingly limitless postwar growth and expansion of economic security to an era of displacement, confusion, and homage to "the market." Of the vague, by no means comforting latter-day mantra "globalization," and of brittle, transient boom times. Behind them, of the fin-de-siècle realities of "downsizing," the swelling "temp" workforce, and anxiety about social security by whatever name. Of the breaking of the chain that bound so many Americans to the ongoing story — the news — of national progress.[7]

Writ larger still, it may be argued, the story is the spectacle of modern civilization gone over the top, even as the West "wins" the Cold War: nuclear and chemical weapon proliferation; the resurgence of tribal nationalisms; AIDS, the lethal postscript to sexual liberation; back-from-the-dead bacteria more powerful than the postwar wonder drugs; worldwide communication systems screaming with the "entertainment" of violence and nihilism; cities as battlefields, choking on dysfunction . . .

But that's too much for any but a postmodern, post-gonzo mind to handle: an apocalypse. If that's what modernity run amok adds up to, it exceeds the abilities of a newsroom or a news business, for it challenges civilization itself. So pull back to the milder phenomenon of American alienation in our time: to the widely documented falloff in engagement with news and participation in politics at the voting booth, to the erosion of hope and optimism and rise of dead-end cynicism, on the part of millions and millions of American people.

IV

SOME WORKING PREMISES: Almost all recent writers on politics and on journalism have focused more or less separately on what ails one or the other. But neither can be understood today except in the context of the dense intertwinings of the one *to* the other. The cultures as well as the machinery of politics and journalism were always linked, and later interactive. Indeed, in an earlier period of concern about that linkage — after World War I and the emergence of propaganda and modern mass media — Walter Lippmann asserted, "The present crisis of western democracy is a crisis in journalism."[8]

But, for reasons to be explored, the effects of politics and the press upon each other today are much more powerful than in the past. And the relationships are more interwoven, now a maze of manipulations, now extremes of demonization, both evident as base scandal consumed Washington in 1998. As in the most dangerous of relationships — conspiracy, incest — some of those behavior patterns on the part of press and political players have evolved into pathology.[9]

Second, the complexities of the drama do not end there. The evolving story of the intertwined cultures of politics and journalism today is, as stated above, part of a larger American narrative. Admittedly, no phase of a nation's history can be generalized about without omission of significant countertrends. The forces at work in the years in which the United States was riding high, from the 1940s almost through the 1960s, of course included a number that were regressive, discordant, and destructive. Nevertheless, for the purpose of untangling the riddles of contemporary press and political dysfunction, consider the larger historical narrative of the first several postwar decades in the terms in which most politicians and the mainstream press have told the story, and the great mass of the public has heard it: the grand, symbolic labels and shorthand that attached to those years, in fact as well as myth . . . The American Century . . . The Postwar American Dream . . . Leadership of the Free World . . .

The theses of such scholars as Paul Kennedy in *The Rise and Fall of the Great Powers* and Michael Sandel in *Democracy's Discontent* about what happened next may be disputed, and there are of course many important ways in which the situation of Americans today, especially women and minorities, is much to be preferred to what it was forty, thirty, and even twenty-five years ago. Nevertheless, allowing for the counterindications, think of the main line of the story of America since the late 1960s as that of transit from a time and a sense of heroic national accomplishment and optimism to the dissolution of that time and sense. Such a troubled passage in national identity together with the general failure of political and journalistic leadership to deal with it guarantees failures of comprehension, mistaken diagnosis, and poorly aimed accusations; no end of confusion.

Third, I find few villains and heroes in this drama. Many if not most of us who have worked in journalism or in politics and government in the past three decades have been troubled by the slide away from truth telling in public discourse. Some have been troubled enough to make some noise, take some meager action. Yet we who have labored there also bear responsibility for what has come to be, and not just because it's the American nature to adapt and manage rather than to protest and make revolutions.

Richard Hofstadter and others have interpreted the American political tradition as pragmatic, adaptive to middle-class discontents but not to genuine radicalism. American journalism, not so differently, worked as successfully as it did for decades because of its proximity to the mainstream. At the turn of the century, with class protest on the rise, the preference of the press was for noisy crusades against slum conditions and corrupt politicians, not for appeals to revolutionary ideologies. Both American politics and American journalism knew when to run ahead of the tide of protest. Hence the teaming of political Progressivism and journalistic muckraking. Hence FDR's matching of his congressional and administrative New Deal strategies with adroit advocacy of them through newspapers, magazines, radio, and newsreels — and their accommodation of FDR even though their owners hated him. Hence, for more than a decade, the progress of a civil rights movement in which activist Supreme Court decisions, legislation, and courageous journalism worked in tandem with and even ahead of mass demonstrations and protest.

Ideological journalism, "to the barricades," and à bas the opposition was for Europe and other continents. In the United States the press was handed the opportunity to ride the urban, communications, production, and transportation revolutions of the late nineteenth century into the era of mass media on the vast national canvas. Allowing for fire-eaters here and there, the operational instincts of the American press tended to follow those of Lincoln and Roosevelt: to right wrongs and support the Union in ongoing fashion in the broadest sense; to apply pragmatic means to the challenges of spreading opportunity and making the system work better.

THERE IS ALSO the overriding enormity and the inertia of modern institutional life. In journalism, the imperative is to perform one's craft and calling well against daily deadlines and the more recent and threatening marketplace pressures, and to leave the meaning of it all to those who neither practice the profession nor bear the responsibility. In politics and government today, the imperative is to win or at least cope, even if the means to that end stink worse and worse.

And therein lies the dilemma, and one of the circumstances for the slide down. For in journalism, the maintenance of any kind of honesty and integrity depends on professionalism — in ideal form, the never ending Socratic back and forth between critical skepticism on one hand, and fairness and balance on the other. The tension between the two sets of values plays out within responsible journalists' heads, in newsrooms, between the press and the subjects of its coverage, between the press and its audiences. As we shall see, the fact that as many of the country's news organizations have continued to put out as high a quality of journalism as they do in the face of their managers' confusion, inconstancy, and retrenchment, and in the context of such political and cultural disintegration, is a credit to that professionalism.

Indeed, putting the matter of passion or even ideology aside (in fact, many successful American journalists have those on the side), the men and women of the press tend to serve us best when they anchor themselves in professional norms. That means accepting the limits of journalism's ability, ultimately, to know, and in news stories, ultimately to judge. Experimentation with such modes of reporting and writing as adventure, investigation, anthropology, history, impressionism, satire, and, in various circumstances, advocacy are among journalism's resources in rising from formulaic hackwork to the realms of courage and critical intelligence. But its practitioners tend to get into trouble when they cross the line from reporting, insightful analysis, and evocative writing to professional roles distinct from the ones they're paid (or licensed) to perform — such as undercover law enforcement officer, prosecutor, court of law, psychiatrist, or fabulist. So two cheers for professionalism.

Chugging along under deadline pressure, journalistic professionalism for its part blends well with kibitzing and surface reform, but not with radical challenge. (As I will argue, the movement advertising itself as pathbreaking — "civic journalism" — is at best only half a concept.)

But alas, that professionalism, resilient though it is, is today a mere subset of a mammoth, proliferating multimedia news, information, and entertainment industry. And that gargantuan media enterprise is itself too much a combine of engine and inertia, too big and relentless, its modus operandi too focused on the immediate, to foster the capacity to stop, cold, and think, profoundly.

The prevailing situation in a political system bereft of substance and overwhelmed by marketing imperatives is as bad or worse. The early retirement in disgust on the part of a wave of elected officials of integrity in recent years suggests greater readiness to protest trends in the political sphere than in the journalistic — but no more successful remedial action.

I was a journalist from 1963 to 1986, for most of those years at *The Atlantic Monthly* and *The Boston Globe*, for a number of them as a managing editor, and for my last fifteen months at the *Globe* as editor-in-chief. Before that and along the way I had staff positions — first in the office of the U.S. Senate majority leader, then in the office of the secretary of state — that gave me privileged views of politics and government. I can't claim that, had I stayed in journalism or returned to government after 1986, I would have done much better than my most admired professional colleagues in pushing back against the forces examined in these pages. The instinct and freedom to do so in more than marginal ways don't go with the business of fighting the good fight day by day.

MORE SIGNIFICANT THAN individual performance has been an environment and a rooted set of behavior patterns much more determining than any player or players. I don't see the issue so much as fixing blame in the present (though there's enough to go around), but rather of comprehending context and process. What was the history that shaped the present? How to respond to the riddles scholars wrestle with: nature, or nurture? Chicken, or egg? Overriding, direct cause, or multiple, indirect effect?

Finding answers to such riddles is the more difficult because computer-driven technologies have spawned ever so many more clever efficiencies, but ever so much less wisdom. As market values and electronics have come to dominate the way we live, the tools of quantification, measurement, communication, and targeting are ever so much more supple — even as they play with those who employ them. So the combined force of those techniques has equipped politicians and the press to identify, segment and reach audiences as never before — and (chicken or egg?) converged with a trend toward trivialization in what they deliver to those audiences. The refinement to the nth power of the arts of manipulation of image and symbol is evident in (chicken or egg?) the displacement of the theory and practice of leadership of opinion by the theory and practice of marketing to it.

And cause and effect? Harvard political scientist Robert D. Putnam, author of an influential essay about the decline of civic engagement and social connectedness in the United States called "Bowling Alone," argues elsewhere that social science research points to television, which "privatizes leisure time," as a central "culprit" in the erosion of civic community in America. Putnam is persuasive, but social science is contentious, and as his searching analysis continues to take shape it has been and will be contested.[10]

For our purposes in this search, suffice it to say that television ascended to dominance in modern culture more or less simultaneously — and interactively — with the rollout of other powerful agents and transforming processes of change in this country, some for the good, some not, some double-edged. They are as various as suburbanization, the Vietnam War, Watergate, computer technology, inflation; industrial, trade, and currency crises; the antiestablishment social, cultural, racial, gender, and institutional revolutions of the 1960s and 1970s; and of course more . . . As we shall see, the causes and effects join, mix, and turn as in a frenzied dance to the millennium.

THE SUBJECT MATTER woven together here spreads across a complex and far-flung terrain: the dynamics and timelines of transformations of press and politics in the United States from the postwar era to the present. Distinct pieces of that terrain are the focus of many more thorough studies. I refer to a number of them but don't wish to re-cover the ground they've been over.

But almost no study exists that even attempts to capture the whole. My goal is not to do so in encyclopedic fashion, and I don't claim to have done it in scientific fashion. Here I readily distance myself from some of the social scientists who have written on these subjects, particularly on the press, too often in the absence of first-hand experience of their subject matter, too often as if their statistical data were the beginning and end of larger realities. Instead, based on my own idiosyncratic experience of politics and journalism, my goal is to develop a thesis about the whole as well as the parts, the better to suggest the relations among them. It's to suggest, again based on that experience, how overwhelming is the weight of evidence that Americans are in the eye of a storm — a democratic crisis in a republic of denial — that is the more threatening because of helplessness to date in coming to terms with it.

PART 1

As We Were

ONE

"Let's Remember the Energy"

AMERICANS' PASSAGE FROM an era of cohesive, heroic national enterprise, fortune, and spirit to times in which alienation, pessimism, loss, and disintegration became rampant is a story sensed and even known in the streets, among friends and co-workers, in families. Novelists and playwrights wrestle with it. But the story of that passage is not for the most part the subject of political or journalistic discourse.

Save for an interlude in the 1970s, neither political leadership nor mainstream journalism have been able to name or contend with the story in a sustained and comprehensive way, for a fundamental reason. Full articulation of it — it is understood in politics and the news business — backfires with bedrock constituencies and audiences, giving them more harsh news when what they want is relief from it. This anxiety about giving offense is also part of the story. So the story, and the taboo attaching to it, have fed upon each other. Thus, a sizable part of the full story of our time has, over the long haul, with some honorable exceptions, been more or less officially unspeakable.

That politicians should avoid forcing full discussion of so painful a story on a resistant public is not new or surprising. They behaved similarly with respect to slavery in the United States in the decades preceding the Civil War, and toward totalitarian dictators' designs abroad through the 1930s.

That the press as a whole should have missed the story in our time is another matter. For the modern press renewed its vows in recent decades to note, question, investigate, connect, correct, critique, fill in, that which officials and politicians celebrate, claim, charge, conceal, overlook, evade, deny, wish, pretend, and actually do.

TO UNRAVEL THIS state of unreason, and perpetuation of it by those in command of public discourse, fall back to the key turning points on the road to today's confusion.

Six months before Pearl Harbor, with isolationism still a force in the land and President Roosevelt still a very cautious internationalist, the most influential publisher in the country, a Republican, preempted center stage in the national debate. Condemning "the moral and practical bankruptcy of any and all forms of isolationism," Henry Luce used the pages of his popular *Life* magazine to declare the era "the American Century." He called for an end to Americans' failure "to play their part as a world power — a failure which has had disastrous consequences for themselves and for all mankind. And the cure is this: to accept wholeheartedly our duty and our opportunity as the most powerful and vital nation in the world and in consequence to exert upon the world the full impact of our influence, *for such purposes as we see fit and by such means as we see fit*" (emphasis added).

Why would such a posture not simply replace Europe's fading imperialism with our own? Because in this "revolutionary" century, said Luce, America was the world's premier democracy. Our newfound world role, he exhorted, "must be a sharing with all people of our Bill of Rights, our Declaration of Independence, our Constitution, our magnificent industrial products, our technical skills. It must be an internationalism of the people, by the people, for the people."[1]

VICTORY IN World War II was a triumph not only for American arms and the American political system. The American economy, converting industry to build the arms, overwhelmed the German and Japanese mobilization machines, wiping out unemployment at home and thus the residue of the Great Depression. The war left the nation, alone among the principal participants, resilient in victory.

America, it was universally agreed, had "come of age," with morale and will to match the national muscle.[2]

It was a victory, along with the rest, for lessons learned. Franklin Roosevelt, Harry Truman, and the men around them, veterans of disillusion and dislocation in the wake of World War I, orchestrated a post–New Deal, postwar consensus supporting "full employment" and economic growth.[3]

At home, American victory in the war was a boon for pluralism. Labor took wartime and postwar hits, but it was a player as never before in party politics, in generating social policy, and in negotiation with industry, and it was growing stronger. With their fair-employment-practices initiatives and gradual racial integration of the armed services, Presidents Roosevelt and Truman commenced the second post–Civil War Reconstruction.[4]

Other groups basked in the warmth of postwar American pluralism and prosperity. The G.I. Bill of Rights served younger veterans' educational aspirations, housing, and credit needs. The boom in modern household appliances began to free women from the unrelenting hard labor of housekeeping. The United States' determining role in the creation of Israel in 1948 recognized a devastated world Jewry and, implicitly, American Jews as well. Passionate grass-roots participation in both the Eisenhower and the Stevenson campaigns of 1952 refreshed and renewed the Republican and Democratic parties.

The narrator of Philip Roth's *American Pastoral* creates a verbal documentary of the soaring spirit of the time:

> Let's remember the energy. Americans were governing not only themselves but some two hundred million people in Italy, Austria, Germany, and Japan. The war-crimes trials were cleansing the earth of its devils once and for all. Atomic power was ours alone. Rationing was ending, price controls were being lifted; in an explosion of self-assertion . . . laborers by the millions demanded more and went on strike for it. And playing Sunday morning softball . . . and pickup basketball on the asphalt courts behind the school were all the boys who had come back alive, neighbors, cousins, older brothers, their pockets full of separation pay, the GI

Bill inviting them to break out in ways they could not have imagined possible before the war. . . . And the upsurge of energy was contagious. Around us nothing was lifeless. Sacrifice and constraint were over. . . . Everything was in motion. The lid was off. Americans were to start over again, en masse, everyone in it together.[5]

An almost ecclesiastical version of such spirit can be found toward the end of Dean Acheson's audaciously titled memoir of his years at the center of foreign policy making, *Present at the Creation*. Summarizing the postwar American realpolitik he and his colleagues had shaped, Acheson wrote:

These lines of policy, which have guided the actions of our country for nearly two decades, were not sonorous abstractions — much less what President Lincoln called "pernicious abstractions" — written down in a sort of official book of proverbs. Nor were they rules or doctrines. Rather they were precedents and grew by the method of the Common Law into a *corpus diplomaticum*. . . . Its central aim and purpose was to safeguard the highest interest of our nation, which was to maintain as spacious an environment as possible in which free states might exist and flourish. Its method was common action with like-minded states to secure and enrich the environment and to protect one another from predators through mutual aid and joint effort.[6]

Popular culture reflected a more informal application of these policies. *Call Me Madam,* Irving Berlin's hit musical comedy of 1950, featured Ethel Merman in a role modeled on the Truman administration's party-giving "hostess with the mostess on the ball," Perle Mesta. Truman rewarded Mesta with the ambassadorship to Luxembourg, at the heart of the postwar European industrial recovery. On Broadway, Merman as "Ambassador Sally Adams" sang an ode to the Europeans based on American Marshall Plan and Point Four aid:

Can you use any money today . . .
Nice new bills that we're giving away . . .
Can you use any dollars today . . .
We've so much that it gets in our way.

JOURNALISM'S ROLE AT the level of opinion making and commentary in those years was, more often than not, a reflection and interpretation of these grand story lines. The press of course gave time and space to those who questioned the story — Henry Wallace and others on the left, Robert Taft, Joseph McCarthy, Richard Nixon, and others on the right. Walter Lippmann, at the center, challenged elements of the Truman administration's evolving policies to contain Soviet designs in Europe and the Near East. But even in a critical posture the press was driven less by the hard-bitten, reflex skepticism common today than by a more or less idealistic view that great nations performing great deeds should be held to the highest standards. "We can do better," said the press at such moments.

Covering the organizing sessions of the United Nations in San Francisco in 1945 for *The New Yorker*, E. B. White paused on the conduct of American reporters observing Allied diplomats' solicitousness toward nations notoriously sympathetic to the Axis powers in the late war.

> Argentina was on the fire and [U.S. Secretary of State Edward] Stettinius was being backed against the wall and made to explain how a peace-loving nation could also be a Fascist-loving nation, and vice versa. A good many newspaper people, that day, were sore right up to their armpits, and although they were present in the capacity of recorders . . . they were extending their function and were managing, in the course of asking questions, to make short, hot speeches from the floor. Thus the Press, in the process of being told, was right in there telling. It was a fascinating moment in the pungent laboratory of democracy, with test tubes and flashbulbs exploding with a cosmic crackle.[7]

But on the whole journalism followed its leaders: elite, insider reporters and commentators like Lippmann and Arthur Krock, and later James Reston and the Alsop brothers. And allowing for deviations, they tended to follow *their* leaders. That is, the work of journalism's peers was shaped as well as informed by the culture of power as conducted in world capitals, especially Washington. ("Hark, *The Herald Tribune* sings, Walter Lippmann's dined with kings," went some doggerel of the time.) Roosevelt, Truman, Eisenhower, and their top national security advisers saw those premier reporters and commentators as interlocutors, sometimes as friends; but more important, however edgily, as collaborators — by which I don't mean stooges — in a long-term project. That project was the steady growth in America's leadership role in the world as the twentieth century unfolded. At home, it was the steady extension of the national agenda, and — allowing for swings between Democratic and Republican emphasis — the *government's* dual agenda. That was, first, stabilizing and reforming the ravaged economy in the 1930s, regulating and fueling it thereafter, and second, the expansion of opportunity and betterment of social conditions.

The relationship between thoughtful men in power and thoughtful men in the press (with rare exceptions they were of course all men) was not necessarily one of co-optation of the journalists. Indeed, the traffic could run the other way. Lippmann, as Sidney Blumenthal has written, "descended from his lofty tower and involved himself with the decision-makers, advising them and writing speeches for them, putting his words into their mouths. . . . He was on intimate terms with politicians and statesmen; he could be influenced, of course, but he liked to think that the others were serving him and his imperial column."[8]

There were strong disagreements — over Cold War policymaking, over the creation of Israel, over Europe-first versus Asia-first policies, over nuclear policy, over the direction of the economy. But the shared view among peers of government and peers of the press was that America's responsibilities had never been greater. It followed that for those at the top who traded intimately with one another in privileged information, the need for the press to assist in public education about those awesome new national responsibilities had never been more urgent.

As a principal architect of postwar foreign policy, Acheson was, as his biographer notes, "careful to cultivate certain journalists." Chief among them was James Reston of *The New York Times*. As Reston recalled the basis of the relationship in his memoirs, "if you're looking for a decisive point in the politics of the twentieth century — the emergence of the United States from isolation to the protection of

Western civilization—the place and time are Washington in the late forties and early fifties, and Acheson, in my view, was the central figure in the drama."[9]

THAT WORLD, VIEWED from the end of the century, was of course clubby and narrow. On the other hand, a common observation of our time is that where giants walked then, midgets pose now.

Henry Luce, upstaging the nation's leaders with *The American Century,* helping to bankroll Winston Churchill out of office in the 1940s, set the tone, but he was hardly alone. Ben Bradlee, legendary editor of *The Washington Post,* recalls in his memoirs a formative experience in his cub reporter days, covering a race riot in the summer of 1949 over segregated swimming pools in the District of Columbia, then still administered by the U.S. Department of the Interior. Bradlee filed a vivid report. That evening in the newsroom, he searched for his story in the first edition of the next day's paper and found it played way down, cleansed of alarming details, and buried way inside. Bradlee exploded with "indignation about how the great liberal *Washington Post* was scared to tell the truth." Just then he received a tap on the shoulder from publisher Philip Graham, dressed in a tuxedo. "All right Buster," said Graham, "come on up with me."

In Graham's office were Truman's secretary and undersecretary of the interior and White House counsel Clark Clifford, all, like Graham, in tuxedos, engaged in something other than the usual stag dinner retreat. The publisher commanded his reporter to tell the officials what in fact had happened that afternoon, thanked him, and sent him back to the newsroom. Graham then told the group, Bradlee later learned, that either the pools would be closed and reopened the next year, integrated, or Bradlee's "real" story would run on page one of the newspaper the next day.

A done deal—but as Bradlee wrote, "a deal no publisher would make today." In her own memoirs Graham's widow Katharine calls the deal "a typical example of the way Phil used power, in this case the paper's, to accomplish something good," but calls it not "appropriate" to "keep a story out of the paper to achieve a purpose, even a fine one."[10]

Ben Bradlee and Kay Graham both salute contemporary standards for separating the truth-telling role of the press from its potential for flexing its muscles behind the scenes. But both pass over the historical fact that in those days, a sense of common purpose, and not just the thrill of power, often joined those in charge of government and those in charge of the press as comrades-in-arms.

The men in Graham's office that night were each, after all, committed liberals struggling with a mockery of justice in the capital of the nation that led the free world, still almost a decade away from coming to terms with its racial segregation. The meeting's point man was the same Clark Clifford who had, the previous year, engineered Truman's come-from-behind strategy as the first out-and-out civil rights candidate for president of the United States in history. It was not that Graham, for his part, was brazenly bending government to *The Washington Post*'s will. It was that he was managing the paper so as to help identify and resolve the great problems of the nation, newly established as leader of the free world, and of its capital, the city in which Graham happened to publish his and his wife's family's newspaper.

IT IS COMMON now to view the postwar era through a darker lens. That was a time (it's argued) of incipient American imperialism, of complacency, narrowness, fear, and reaction, of insensitivity to the aspirations of women and minorities, a time when children grew up haunted by nuclear anxiety and obsession with "the bomb."

The pendulum did swing heavily from reform and hope to reaction and fear in the postwar years. The war buried isolationism, but McCarthyism, mixing anger over Soviet intelligence's penetration of the Roosevelt and Truman administrations together with old nativist furies, unleashed hysteria in the land. It distorted politics and public policies. It ruined careers and lives far beyond the ranks of those the Soviets had compromised.

And the press helped the demagogues. How could that have happened?

The postwar red scare was far along when Senator Joseph R. McCarthy jumped on the issue in February 1950. Alger Hiss had been convicted of perjury for having denied before the House Un-American Activities Committee that he was a Communist three weeks before McCarthy hurled his first charges. HUAC had been in full cry about "communists in government" since 1947, generally in tandem with security agencies that had gotten there much earlier, feeding hysteria but sometimes picking up on what we know now to have been the genuine article.

Most of the press, much more provincial than today, was reliant on the national wire services for news on such fronts and less inclined to make its own judgments about them. And the wire services were frightened of offending clients by appearing to add interpretation, let alone implicit judgment, to word of who said what about whom in a breaking news story.

George Reedy, then a United Press reporter and subsequently press secretary to Lyndon Johnson, observed that Joe McCarthy "couldn't find a Communist in Red Square — he didn't know Karl Marx from Groucho — but he was a United States Senator." McCarthy's sheer brazenness trumped the journalistic norms of the day; as historian Edwin Bayley noted, "editors and editorial writers refused to believe that McCarthy would make such charges without having the evidence to back them up." Therefore, recalled Reedy, "We had to take what McCarthy said at face value. . . . And boy, he really had the press figured out."

McCarthy understood the mechanics and needs of the press, its deadlines and cycles. According to Murray Marder of *The Washington Post*, reporters themselves led McCarthy on, coming to him and saying, " 'I must have a story.' And McCarthy would go through his files until he found something. McCarthy learned that on Friday the wire service reporters were always in need of stories that could be run on Sunday or Monday, the two dead news days, and he saved up tidbits for them." William Theis of the International News Service summed it up this way: "We let Joe [McCarthy] get away with murder, reporting it as he said it, not doing the kind of critical analysis we'd do today. All three wire services were so God damned objective that McCarthy got away with everything, bamboozling the editors and the public. It was a sad period in American journalism."[11]

A remarkable benediction came early on from none other than Dean Acheson, a lightning rod for attacks by McCarthy as a coddler of Communists. In a talk to the American Society of Newspaper

Editors at the outset of McCarthy's rampage in 1950, the secretary of state said, "Now, I don't ask for your sympathy. I don't ask you for help. You are in a worse situation than I am. I and my associates are only the intended victims of this mad and vicious operation. But you, unhappily, you by reason of your calling, are participants. You are unwilling participants, disgusted participants, but nevertheless, participants, and your position is far more serious than mine."[12]

The recovery was slow (and the press all too slow in moving to more interpretive reporting), but the terror eased. Responsible politicians and some journalists pushed back. Television itself helped; the Army-McCarthy hearings before a Senate committee caught McCarthy at his most reckless and devious for all to see. In turnabout, McCarthy himself was censured in the Senate, and ruined.

To see the era only through a dark, revisionist lens is to miss the overall exuberant mood of the nation as a whole, still riding the wave of victory in World War II. The immensely popular President Eisenhower's winning campaign slogan, "Peace and Prosperity," was a formulation with which there was little fundamental quarrel.

AMERICANS' FAITH IN progress, notwithstanding the ravages of anti-Communist hysteria and nuclear anxiety, maintained and even renewed itself. Revisionism on the left, in the spirit of C. Wright Mills, paints public policy up through Vietnam as a case of indiscriminate, unthinking anti-Communism, unable to heed Eisenhower's valedictory warning about a growing military-industrial complex. War, in Mills's bitter words (echoing George Orwell's in *Nineteen Eighty-Four*), was "no longer an interruption of peace; in our time, peace itself has become an uneasy interlude between wars; peace has become a perilous balance of mutual terror and mutual fright."[13]

But that leaves out the determination to avoid the selfish folly of the 1920s and blind denial of the rise of fascism in the 1930s. It leaves out the then prevalent idea that what the country was about was the measured, pragmatic application of American know-how, American idealism and will — the still-ripe fruit of 1945. If (went the governing consensus) there was a threat abroad — and there were threats, in Europe, in competition for the new weaponry of destruction, in espionage—they would be, and were, met. As in Luce's articulation of an "American Century," the ideology underlying that resolve was informed as much by the liberal internationalism of the time as by anti-Communism.

At home, with the exception of the Taft-Hartley Act's check on organized labor's new power, the flow of social and economic legislation through the Truman and Eisenhower years was generally in the direction of expansive outlay and liberal reforms. The spirit of the times was that what *was* repressive, inequitable, or an affront to the American dream—bad schools, slums, failing farms, poor health care, disease itself—required in the way of remedy only the naming of the wrong, and then the focusing of legislation, expertise, energy, and money on it.

As to civil rights (and also civil liberties, despite the toll taken by McCarthyism), the Supreme Court in the "complacent" Eisenhower years expanded definitions of freedom and equality at their very roots. The Democratic-led Congress under Ike passed federal aid to education bills, legislation to build hospitals, clear slums, and construct modern housing for working- and middle-class families, support farm prices, build public power systems, lay out a modern national highway system, fund research into dread diseases. Congress even beat down reactionary efforts to roll back libertarian Supreme Court decisions in the late 1950s, though sometimes by the narrowest of margins.[14]

By 1957, when the ambitious Senate majority leader, Lyndon B. Johnson of Texas, broke the Southern-dominated congressional blockade against civil rights legislation that had prevailed since the end of the first Reconstruction, no category for the national agenda was inadmissible. Even in the United States' bastion of reaction— the racially segregated South—the shrewdest of white leaders, such as Senator Richard Russell of Georgia, saw change coming and acquiesced in behind-the-scenes accommodations with it (if not, like Johnson, going so far as to help it along).[15]

THE PRESS ATTITUDE toward those who governed through the midcentury decades has been described as reverential, but such terminology also misses the point. The attitude was closer to trust—

discounting for the usual roguish behavior and thievery, as on the part of Harry Truman's "Missouri Gang." Trust, because the overall story line was that the system worked. Americans had reason to trust a government that appeared to be in overdrive in bringing them progress, in the form of expanded education, housing and medical programs, cheap credit, higher minimum wages, and more job security. Undergirding all these, defining "the American dream," was the seemingly boundless postwar consumer economy. Even the boundaries of the nation swelled; in 1959 Hawaii and Alaska become the forty-ninth and fiftieth states.[16]

As late as 1965 journalist Meg Greenfield could write (tongue-in-cheek, reflecting a still-confident mood in Washington) that the can-do Johnson administration was alarmed that a "solution explosion" was leading to "an unprecedented problem drain." Greenfield's jest was bemused rather than sarcastic, reflecting identification on the part of the mainstream press with the optimistic spirit of the times. But as the tide of American mastery of its challenges crested, Greenfield's telling send-up of 1965 quickly became a dated period piece.[17]

TWO

And Then . . .

THE UPHEAVALS IN American circumstances and consciousness that began in the 1960s were simultaneous, and in part interwoven, with radical transformation of the ways society exchanges information about such epic change. For television and then the computer, a "communications revolution" driving its own imperatives and effects and prompting others, landed smack in the middle of a modern American society experiencing political, economic, and cultural upheaval. Thus, what constituted the press began to change at its core just about the time the story line it was telling — the nature and content of the news — began to change at *its* core.

The dislocating events and forces at work in the 1960s and 1970s are individually well known and need not be rehearsed in detail here. But consider briefly how they piled in on one another, in accelerated sequence, adding up to much more than the sum of the parts.

The deployment of American power abroad begins to backfire

U.S.-backed coups in Iran and Guatemala in the early 1950s, like the bluster of John Foster Dulles about use of nuclear weaponry, stretched but did not crack the broad postwar foreign policy consensus. But in the 1960s, against the backdrop of the end of colonialism, American subversion of leftist regimes and insurgencies in the Third World began to look futile and embarrassing. The Kennedy administration's disaster at Cuba's Bay of Pigs set the discordant tone.

The heirs to the architects of allied victory in World War II and of the rebuilding of postwar Europe and Japan had devised a new stratagem, which they called "counterinsurgency." But critics conjured up images of quicksand and quagmire wars, and in the name of freedom and security they derided American alliances with the right-wing dictators of the world.

Into the solid consensus supporting postwar American internationalism, and "leadership of the free world" through grand schemes like the Marshall Plan and NATO, crept doubts about the United States' uses of its power abroad.

A time of consensus gives way to a time of expanded rights and social change, of iconoclasm and ferment

May 1, 1960: The contraceptive pill hit the market; more than 400,000 women were using it by the end of 1961.

June 1962: A convention of Students for a Democratic Society in Port Huron, Michigan, noting that "the dreams of the older left were perverted by Stalinism," called for "truly democratic alternatives to the present" and issued "New Left" guidelines for radical action.

1962: Rachel Carson's alarming *Silent Spring* helped sow the seeds of an environmental protest movement.

1963: Betty Friedan's *The Feminine Mystique* became the bible of a vital women's movement determined to settle for nothing less than full equality between the sexes.

August 28, 1963: Leaders of the civil rights movement, frustrated by brutal responses to nonviolent demonstrations and attempts to attain basic rights in the South, and by the slow pace of federal government response to civil rights demands, moved north. The March on Washington signaled a shift in the politics of race from debates and demonstrations about rights to assertions of power.

February 1964: The Beatles landed in New York; a "counterculture" took wing.[1]

The living-room assassination

November 22, 1963: The shock of the assassination of President Kennedy in the streets of Dallas, Texas, a center of right-wing fervor, reverberated through a hypnotically powerful new medium. Television — in 92 percent of American homes that year, compared with 55 percent ten years earlier — had arrived as the vehicle of mass communication. Television covered the assassination of Kennedy's assassin on November 25, in the hands of the Dallas police, live.

President Lyndon Johnson, himself an inevitable subject of crackpot speculation about involvement in Kennedy's death, gave strong private credence to theories of Cuban and even Vietnamese complicity in the assassination. But he moved quickly to organize an official response that suppressed such questions in order to calm the waters.

Not the least important outcome: the launching of a feverish American conspiracy-theory industry.

A "Great Society" explodes in urban race riots

Cruel fate for a passionate devotee of Rooseveltian policies. Like FDR in the wake of his own apprenticeship to Woodrow Wilson, Lyndon Johnson was determined to go his mentor one better, striding forth where the New Deal had merely groped. He would sweep poverty and injustice from the land and generate new boom times on a great wave of consensus-supported public spending and social reorganization.

But on the heels of Johnson's achievements of historic civil rights legislation and of moral force as a national leader, the streets of Watts in Los Angeles and Harlem in New York, of Detroit, Washington, and other cities, began exploding in rage.

The season of reform and brotherhood was glorious and brief. Neither Johnson nor Martin Luther King nor their allies could hold the line for a politics of racial consensus. The rhetoric of racial integration gave way to that of black power and white backlash.

And the latest presidential prophet of the American dream was on his way to becoming the protagonist in an American tragedy.

Escalation

The Kennedy assassination came just three weeks after the coup against the South Vietnamese government that included the execution of President Ngo Dinh Diem, a coup approved by senior Kennedy administration officials. Then:

August 2, 1964: Murky reports of naval engagements off the coast of North Vietnam . . . August 7: The Gulf of Tonkin Resolution authorizing all measures deemed necessary by the commander in chief against further attacks on the armed forces of the United States flew through Congress with only two dissenting votes . . .

February 6, 1965: A Viet Cong attack on a U.S. base at Pleiku in South Vietnam prompted a retaliatory U.S. air attack on a North Vietnamese base . . . February 8: Systematic American bombing of North Vietnam commenced . . .

March 24, 1965: Antiwar protests had hitherto been marginal. At the University of Michigan, forty-nine faculty members and three thousand students debated American action in Vietnam in an all-night "teach-in." Teach-ins followed quickly at Columbia (twenty-five hundred participants), Berkeley (twenty thousand participants), and more than a hundred other campuses.

April 17, 1965: Fifteen thousand demonstrators picketed the White House to protest American action in Vietnam . . .[2]

Meanwhile, a New Deal for the press . . .

On September 2, 1963, CBS, and a week later NBC, moved from fifteen-minute "talking-head" evening news programs to a thirty-minute format employing film and action. The pace at which television would supplant print journalism accelerated.

(The expansion of the evening news broadcast coincided with reports of American pressure on the repressive Diem regime in South Vietnam. To "demonstrate his interest in more extensive news coverage," as *The New York Times* put it, President Kennedy granted Walter Cronkite an interview for the inaugural thirty-minute broadcast. "In the final analysis," said Kennedy delphically to Cronkite, the Vietnam War is "their" — the Vietnamese's — "war. They're the ones who have to win it or lose it.")[3]

On March 9, 1964, the Supreme Court handed down its unanimous decision in *New York Times v. Sullivan,* decreeing that under the First Amendment to the Constitution it was virtually impossible to libel a public figure in the United States. The decision dramatically expanded the real and perceived freedom of the American press. It swept away as well the lingering question whether the Constitution sanctioned suppression of press or speech as "seditious libel" in time of national peril.

(The Court's epic opinion in *Times v. Sullivan* coincided with growing press curiosity about the actual state of affairs in Vietnam. The news was of the Johnson administration's dismay about instability in Vietnam: the coup-makers of November 1963 had themselves been overthrown in January. Reports flowing from Defense Secretary Robert McNamara's trip to Vietnam in March allowed that "United States officials were saying privately that the prospects of defeating the Vietcong were slight or negligible," but McNamara claimed the picture was brighter than published reports would have it. On the NBC magazine show *Sunday,* he announced $50 million in new aid for Saigon, and stated that most of the 15,500 American troops in Vietnam — not yet in combat — would be out by the end of 1965.)[4]

... and a new kind of news

This was the press that all but fought World War II at the side of American fighting men and leaders, reflecting a united public opinion and national resolve. In the postwar years the press reported on the forging of the American "corpus diplomaticum," as Acheson termed it, and in its manner of doing so helped mobilize broad public support for American policies abroad.

But in its coverage of Vietnam, and also of American interventions in the Caribbean in the early 1960s, the press began to report on closely held military policy disputes, to raise questions of its own about them. It was under President Kennedy, not President Nixon, that a press enemies' list came into being, featuring maverick war correspondents. "So you're Browne," Admiral Harry D. Felt greeted Malcolm Browne of the Associated Press at a Saigon press conference in 1962; "why don't you get on the team?" Kennedy followed up by trying (unsuccessfully) to pressure *The New York Times* into pulling Browne's sharp-elbowed colleague in the Saigon press corps, David Halberstam, out of Vietnam.[5]

At home, as the race issue metamorphosed from moral crusade in the South to violent upheaval in the North, television journalists with broadened access to airtime witnessed the discontent; recorded antiwar, anti-establishment demonstrators in the streets and on campuses; filmed a growing caucus of antiwar senators questioning unyielding Johnson administration officials about Vietnam.

Make love, not war

In the background, moving to the fore, alternative culture, counterculture, drop-out culture, commune culture, drug culture. More attitudinal than ideological, "youthquake" proved difficult for the establishment to isolate or confront. It was inclined to deflect political convention; to gather in Woodstock as much as to march on the Pentagon.

"Our work is guided by the sense that we may be the last generation in the experiment with living," wrote Tom Hayden in the Port Huron Statement, alluding to the specter of nuclear apocalypse. In a wry aside Todd Gitlin of Students for a Democratic Society noted that an emblematic figure for the New Left was the tough-talking Marlon Brando astride a motorcycle in the 1953 film *The Wild One*, responding to the question, "What are you rebelling against?" Brando: "Whadda ya got?"[6]

With the emergence of young novelists like Thomas Pynchon in 1961 and Don DeLillo in 1971, artistic postmodernism took a fresh turn — hip paranoia and ironic subversion of mainstream reality, word of culture gone haywire, grimly hilarious visions of breakdown.

1968: Collapse of the mighty, street theater of confrontation, live on TV

Instability, multiplied by the impact of live television, was the order of the day.

On the main stage, disaster in Vietnam and a disintegrating political base at home forced Johnson in effect to resign the presidency in March 1968. It was the season of guerrilla mystique, protest power; then, with the assassinations of Martin Luther King and Robert Kennedy, of anarchy.

Johnson and the party barons, retaining enough power to shut out the antiwar movement at the Democratic National Convention in Chicago in August, failed to factor in the explosive potential of protest in combination with on-site live television coverage. The cameras captured the rage in the convention hall, and the Chicago policemen's violence against protesters outside it; and, more to the point, against the press. For Mayor Richard Daley's police smashed witnessing cameras along with protesters' heads. Television's force, its role in the eyes of the police and their supporters as hostile messengers, partisan and radical, heightened the shock of what seemed for a moment like the onset of civil war.[7]

The party in power had lost control of the issues of war and peace, and law and order, along with that of race. The Democratic Party — the party that from Jefferson to Johnson by way of Roosevelt had defined, redefined, and fought for the aspirations of the American common man — set about reforming itself. But it never recovered from the events of 1968.

The routinization of violence

Symptoms of sickness: guns and crime, gangs and gang war, city streets as free-fire zones. Black Panthers, armed "to defend . . . our black community from racist police oppression and brutality." Armed takeovers of campuses; violence and deaths at Attica and Kent State. Increasingly routine news of consummated and attempted assassinations across the spectrum of racial and political leadership, including those of the Kennedys and King, Malcolm X and George Wallace, Gerald Ford and Ronald Reagan. Later, white racist militias in the outbacks and mountains.[8]

Watergate

Johnson's successor embarked on a bold game plan that included demonization of radicals and liberals and co-optation of white Democratic voters alienated by the events of the 1960s, destroyed himself, and did much to discredit the game.

"The system worked" in exorcising Richard Nixon and Watergate, but it was widely decried as bankrupt. President Ford's pardon of Nixon was "the ultimate cover-up," charged a member of the House Judiciary Committee, and there were editorial-page calls to continue the impeachment process because of the pardon. "What happened [in Watergate] will happen again," said Washington lawyer Lloyd Cutler, later special counsel to President Carter. "The memory of the last few years may very well prevent it from happening for a decade or so, but we all know it will happen again, just as it happened fifty years earlier in the Teapot Dome scandal."[9]

The political parties in receivership

Open primaries and caucuses in every state replaced "the smoke-filled room." But in the name of reform the American two-party political system, with deep roots in communities, families, and homes, always a more tentative, unstable system than the European models and by some measures in decline since the 1920s, was in fact headed for the dustbin. The fight for the 1972 Democratic presidential nomination, noted Mary and Thomas Edsall, "marked the final attempt of the Democratic Party to contain in one tent the range of interest groups that had previously found common ground in support of the traditional Democratic economic liberalism." The new agenda was more centrifugal than common; it highlighted the new identity politics of "black empowerment, women's rights, abortion rights, criminal rights, and issues of personal and sexual liberation." Common cause came in the form of an additional defining issue: party reform.[10]

At the 1972 Democratic convention in Miami, the party's credentials committee, controlled by supporters of Senator George McGovern, threw out Mayor Daley's Chicago delegation, heavy with the old machine-engineered ethnic representation, in favor of a group of reformers organized according to the new race and gender imperatives. "Anybody who would reform Chicago's Democratic Party by dropping the white ethnic would probably begin a diet by shooting himself in the stomach," *The Chicago Daily News*'s earthy Mike Royko remarked. McGovern's spokesman, Frank Manciewicz, echoed Royko: "I think we may have lost Illinois tonight." And lose it for sure McGovern did, with only 40 percent of the vote to Nixon's 59 percent.[11]

For all Nixon's deviousness and instinct to polarize, when he went down he took with him the "Modern Republicanism" of moderation on issues like welfare and the environment, a posture that had brought a Democrat like Daniel Patrick Moynihan to an influential social policy making role in his administration. E. J. Dionne, Jr., of

The Washington Post observed that "the revulsion against Washington that Watergate unleashed . . . played right back into the conservative argument" against the welfare state, and right into the hands of Ronald Reagan, spurring along the triumph of right-wing ideology over pragmatic politics. Thus were both parties "reformed" from engines of consensus into arenas of fragmentation.[12]

America loses a war and pays a price

Experts debated whether we had lost the Vietnam War to Communism, to the forces of Third World nationalism, or to our own miscalculated strategies for Third World intervention.

Anticipating the televised evacuation of the last Americans in Vietnam from the roof of our Saigon embassy, the mighty dollar that helped build postwar stability abroad, badly inflated, gave way as the world's currency standard. The war, defying Washington's assurances that escalation would bring it to a timely conclusion, had never been appropriately financed. Meanwhile the once-devastated Axis powers, recovered with American help, led an upstart charge into world markets, including ours. In 1971, with American industry declining in competitiveness, with trade deficits mounting, President Nixon "floated" the devalued dollar in world currency exchange. No longer banker to the world, the United States would shortly become a debtor nation.

Two years later the Third World declared economic war on the First World. Oil-producing nations embargoed their precious product and quadrupled its price. The West had to choose between responding with force or paying the new price. It paid.

But the nation's overall energy consumption in the 1970s was soaring; it was greater than that of Japan, Britain, Germany, and Russia added together. Shortages of fuel for the engines of modern American life triggered gridlock at the gas pump, price shock, futile efforts at wage-price controls, and uncontainable inflation in a bruised, frustrated, testy United States.[13]

Rustbelt

Economic dislocation at the core blended into the roiled mix of American discontent. The American industrial machine, which when mobilized in World War II had been the key to victory against fascism, was down for the count. "While Japan and Europe had totally rebuilt their steel mills after the war, employing modern technique," wrote historian Donald White, "American companies for the most part continued to operate old facilities until they became uncompetitive and obsolete. Mills closed, throwing laborers out of work."[14]

Discontent with the monotony and displacement of automation was rampant on the assembly line, and quality suffered. *Life* magazine, an upbeat herald of American industrial mobilization in its coverage of the World War II home front, ran a cover story in the summer of 1972 on General Motors' troubled plant in Lordstown, Ohio, headlined "Bored on the Job: Industry Contends with Apathy and Anger on the Assembly Line," with photos emphasizing workers' disaffection. The only automobile ads in that issue of *Life* were for Toyota and Subaru.

A new term of art — "stagflation" — reflected the double bind of inertia and erosion.[15]

Failures of governance

American cities were decaying, their black populations were swelling with migrants from the newly mechanized farms of the South, whites who could afford to were heading for the suburbs, welfare rolls were soaring, crime rates were rising, racial tensions were multiplying, municipal finances were falling apart. Government, solver of problems, was at a loss. The top-down nostrums of previous decades like slum clearance and urban renewal were discredited. The trendier bottom-up one — community action — would become so.

New York, as historian Fred Siegel observed, had "replaced a private sector economy . . . with a public sector economy based on selling its poverty to Washington in return for social service dollars." But this was not a sound arrangement, and when the crunch came in 1975 the New York *Daily News* headline said it all: "FORD TO CITY: DROP DEAD."[16]

For the American steel, auto, aircraft, electronics, and other industries were sick, OPEC was squeezing access to fuel, trade deficits were mounting, inflation was raging, and the American government was not in the enterprising mode. Wars on poverty in the LBJ style, on dread disease, on slums and education, were the victims of their own programmatic shortfalls, feuds among policy advocates, and tightening budgets. In city, state, and national government, the operative words were frustration, paralysis, and higher and higher powered special-interest lobbying for regulatory, tax-code, and subsidy breaks.[17]

Lotteries had helped federal and state governments cover the costs of the Revolutionary and Civil Wars, as well as one-time capital expenditures for education and public works, in the eighteenth and nineteenth centuries. Then they'd faded away. Beginning in the 1970s and then with a computerization-fired vengeance in the 1980s, state after state, hard up for income, facing resistance and even revolt over new or increased taxes, returned to the antique device of the lottery, and then to state-sanctioned casino gambling. This time, the pattern was not short-term investment or financing but permanent funding of state services. Many states, like New York, sugar-coated the new reliance on legalized gambling by earmarking revenue from it for socially worthy categories like education. As time passed, states' reliance on lottery revenue rose. To maintain public participation at the needed levels, the states — addicted themselves — had to raise jackpots higher, and lower their take. Meanwhile, evidence mounted that the lottery was in effect a regressive tax, drawing far more money from poor people looking to get lucky than from the more economically secure.[18]

The end of "the Second Reconstruction"

The politics of race in America turned inside out and rancid, as it had after the Civil War. The blame was shared. Reactionary demagogues exploited white fears of black discontent. As the young Pat Moynihan was among the first to learn, many liberals were quick to label racist the raising of legitimate issues — the disintegration of the black family (the 1965 Moynihan Report's focus), welfare dependency, inner-city crime, and drugs. According to the code of speaking no ill of a brother, many blacks, including leaders like Jesse Jackson, indulged demagogues who blamed the ills of the black underclass on white society, and merchandised race hatred and conspiracy theories to buttress it.

What had once been a heroic, biracial civil rights crusade became an awkward, untrusting game of what Thomas and Mary Edsall called "covert language and . . . coded symbols," a "racially-loaded confrontation over the issue of responsibility, both historic and contemporary," for the situation of black people.[19]

Television begins to fill the vacuum in American politics

When, in the wake of the Democratic Party's disaster of 1968 and the Republican disaster of Watergate, reformers "established a nominating process that is essentially a free-for-all between self-generated candidacies," wrote political scientist Thomas Patterson, "the task of bringing the candidates and voters together . . . was superimposed on a media system that was built for other purposes." Far beyond the confines of the election campaign (the focus of Patterson's study), the American political system was shifting from a party structure built into civil society—"from the courthouse to the White House," as Lyndon Johnson used to say—to an insiders' game in Washington and state capitals, and an ephemeral television show.[20]

Television's currency and forms were images, acting skill, management of the moment, fast cutting in and out of a fragmented visual environment—and entertainment. These supplanted the forms of the old order of national, state, and local politics: radio sound and printed word of landmark speeches, the bustle of hand-shaking, grass-roots, "retail" politics. Videotape, replacing film, made the slicing and splicing of speeches into sound bites that much more efficient. Network evening news sound bites of presidential candidates shrank by 75 percent between 1968 and 1988, from forty-three seconds to nine.

Television news evolved ever more in the direction of what Neil Postman described, long before Disney owned ABC and Time Warner owned CNN, as the orchestration of elements meant to render the news as entertainment: "the good looks and amiability of the cast, their pleasant banter, the exciting music that opens and closes the show, the vivid film footage, the attractive commercials," all suggesting that what's aired, even when it includes "murder and mayhem . . . is no cause for weeping." But the stuff of politics on television — that is, television as the new medium of politics — evolved in more destructive fashion.

Except for the inaccurately termed debates (really stylized press conferences), political content on television was more and more framed in the only format that appeared to arouse a response (albeit a diminishing one): the reductive, vitriolic distortions of the negative advertisement.[21]

THESE WERE SOME of the transforming moments and forces of change in the United States in the 1960s and early 1970s, rolling in one after another, a number of them at once. Bringing word of them to the public was the principal work of the press in those years. Many of them were devastating, the stuff of unspeakable loss. Others — breakthroughs toward true equality for women and minorities, the expansion of definitions of social justice and of freedom of the press, the acknowledgment of the fallibility of hierarchical authority — were positive on their own merits. But many of them added elements of uncertainty and in some cases dislocation and backlash to the mix. Where there were winners, there were losers.

The overall list of these fault lines and transformations could be extended. Little wonder that their mounting effect has been powerful. More curious is that it's been so little recognized politically and journalistically, let alone examined in depth, for the effect it had on the public. But "it" was too diffuse, too anarchic, too dense for such assessment. That part of it that could be managed rhetorically as "the sixties" made a certain amount of shorthand sense — in a manner of speaking, though the phrase resonated variously depending on point of view. But all of it, taken together if that were routinely possible, far exceeded coherence or a shared value system.

EVEN IF "IT" had been clearer, there was a further complicating factor: the assumptions of those doing the reporting and interpreting — that is to say, the state of the news business — began, as we shall see, to unravel.

Some of the upheaval in the news business — aspects of the production, market, and corporate dynamics of the industry — was not a direct function of forces at work on the social and political sphere. But much of it — the public's growing disaffection from the news, the shift from a print to a visual culture — was. The communal consciousness of the Great Depression and then of World War II, highly oriented toward news, was disintegrating. Increasingly, it seemed, people did not want to know, or hear, about a great deal that was happening in modern life.

THREE

Malaise

WITH FEW EXCEPTIONS, mainstream political and journalistic leadership stopped short of offering reflections on this accumulation of national trouble. Conventional wisdom was that America had after all managed its way through other tough challenges in recent times. Indeed many journalists and political leaders persisted in the tones of unquestioned American preeminence that took hold in the postwar years.

Near the peak of the debate about the Vietnam War in 1967–68 the foreign editor of *Newsweek*, a markedly less hawkish news organization than its rival *Time*, echoed officialdom's "one compelling reason" why the United States had to hang in: "The U.S. Government has made so great a commitment in South Vietnam, both in words and in military effort, that failure to achieve our stated objectives there would gravely damage the U.S. position all around the world. It would, more precisely, cast doubt upon the believability of U.S. guarantees and the constancy of U.S. purpose in the eyes of both our allies and our enemies."[1]

In short, noblesse oblige.

Similarly, an establishment argument for the need to close down the Vietnam War — George Ball's and later Clark Clifford's and Dean Acheson's — was that it was a distraction from more pressing American responsibilities in Europe, with NATO, in leadership of the West, in global contest with the Soviet Union. (Charles de Gaulle had told Ball in 1964 that "our position in Vietnam was hopeless," that France's former colony was "rotten country" — *le pays pourri,* as his nation had learned "to its sorrow." His point was that only a very naive great power would confuse its destiny with that of the sorry state of Vietnam.)[2]

Talk of "defeat" at the time was for the purpose of exorcising the thought, as in President Johnson's "I will not be the first American President to lose a war." As late as 1973 *The New York Times* could say in an editorial, "It may not be empty rhetoric to believe that the scars of Vietnam can bring new strength as they heal, strength gathered in a clearer definition of the priorities of the use of national power." But the power of the visual images of the evacuation of the U.S. embassy in Saigon in 1975, marking the failure of thirty years of American policy, exceeded that of such Panglossian words.[3]

FOR A TIME, the rhetoric was upbeat: cleanse the stables, elevate standards, ascend to new heights of national probity. Thus, from the calamitous 1968 Democratic National Convention in Chicago to the fresh air of party and procedural reform. From Watergate to self-congratulatory conclusions that the procedural institutions of the republic (including the press) had saved the day; that strengthening and reform of those institutions would prevent such abuses in the future; that what Gerald Ford called "our long national nightmare" was over.

At the level of the elites, the United States' accumulation of catastrophes did not square with the presumptions of heroic architecture for a great society or leadership of the free world. For the elites, it was time for fundamental reassessment of American assumptions and leadership; not "onward and upward," but "back to school." The titles of books influential among the elites in those years conveyed that theme.

As to America and the world: *The Arrogance of Power,* by J. William Fulbright, 1966; *The Limits of Power,* by Eugene J. McCarthy, 1967; *The Limits of Intervention,* by Townsend Hoopes, 1969; *The Imperial Presidency,* by Arthur M. Schlesinger, Jr., 1973.

Closer to home, *The Death and Life of Great American Cities,* by Jane Jacobs, 1961; *A City Destroying Itself,* Richard J. Whalen on New York, 1965; *The Greening of America,* by Charles Reich, 1970; *Small Is Beautiful,* by E. F. Schumacher, 1973. Christopher

Lasch's acid indictment, *The Culture of Narcissism* (1978), carried the subtitle *American Life in an Age of Diminishing Expectations.*

The Limits to Growth, the Club of Rome's team of MIT scholars called their alarming 1972 report. The product of intense, computer-supported analysis, this document predicted that, "if present growth trends in world population, industrialization, pollution, food production and resource depletion continue unchanged, . . . [t]he most probable result will be a rather sudden and uncontrollable decline in both population and industrial capacity" within the next hundred years. Robert Stobaugh's and Daniel Yergin's influential *Energy Future: Report of the Energy Project at the Harvard Business School* (1979) called the OPEC oil crisis "a warning of a fundamental and dangerous disorder," and framed the sobering case for conservation and development of new energy sources.

Mainstream editorial pages and columnists sometimes echoed the warnings about "running out of everything" and calls for reassessment sounded by the elites. The newsmagazines went further, running cover lines in the late 1970s like "Has America Lost Its Clout?" and — in the midst of the oil embargo, with a cover drawing of a stripped, despondent Uncle Sam — "Over a Barrel."[4]

Richard Nixon blended allusions to that despondency with the wishful exhortations of the varsity coach up against the wall. Disingenuously, he claimed America's painful devaluation of the dollar in 1971 was in fact a bid to "help us snap out of the self-doubt, the self-disparagement that saps our energy and erodes our confidence in ourselves." He asked his audience to answer positively the question "whether this Nation stays number one in the world's economy or resigns itself to second, third or fourth place," and "whether we as a people have faith in ourselves . . . or lose our grip."[5]

Pollsters, politicians, and journalists identified other elements of discontent and trauma, but in fragmented rather than integrated fashion. The "post-Vietnam syndrome" was shorthand for a soured view of the rest of the world and especially of an activist American role in it; together with recrimination against this or that alleged American villain of the Vietnam piece (depending on point of view, the press, "the politicians," or the military).[6]

The rhetoric of urban racial crisis and governmental breakdown was more heated still. Black power advocate Stokely Carmichael denounced "this nonviolent bullshit." The cities adapted themselves to what has been called "riot ideology" — the argument that blame for the mass urban riots of the 1960s was on the backs of white society, and that de facto reparations from government were the only way to keep the peace.[7]

BUT BOTH POLITICAL and journalistic leadership avoided outright acknowledgment that the United States had fallen into a time of crisis and reckoning that demanded truth telling on the order of Churchill's to the British at the worst moments of World War II, or de Gaulle's to the French in 1959 as they endured the loss of their last great piece of empire, Algeria. This was in the nature of the circumstances of the 1970s, more diffuse than those facing Britain in 1940 or France twenty years later.

Then, too, losses for all Americans in the 1960s and 1970s were offset by gains for some. Perception of loss and gain depended in part on one's placement to one or the other side of the tracks of empowerment, and the rhetoric of more liberation to be won was motivational to many. Those who had withdrawn from what they saw as a sick or suffocating American mainstream to form counterculture or New Age communes exuded a positively evangelical and "transformative" energy, reminiscent, as Frances FitzGerald reported, of early-nineteenth-century American utopian communities. The result was a blur, a mix, a mess; part injury, part exhilaration, part hangover.[8]

Meanwhile the trend lines and nature of the reverses defied an assessment of their dimensions taken as a whole. They came and went from the front page. U.S. trade deficits and debtor status became old, and largely impenetrable, news. The energy crisis waned, and so did the demand for sacrifice as in time of war. The newsmagazines went on to the next week, the next cover story, increasingly keyed to trendy "lifestyle" and entertainment topics.

The variety of gains kept alive a reassuring, onward-and-upward story line — the promise of "the American Dream" — including as they did progress for women, black, Latino, and gay people toward fully realized social and economic citizenship; reform and renewal in established institutions; "what will they think of next?" advances in consumer goods and technologies.

But the cumulative meaning of the real reversals as well as the blur of perception of them — the bitter long-term damage to spirit and hope — was lost in the wash for millions of Americans. Consideration of the losses, the virtues of examining America-on-high assumptions, and making sober adjustments had been articulated by the elites, for one another.

No political leader was prepared to take on the new conditions of American life straight out, work through the implications as a matter of urgency to be communicated to the average citizen, and lead the way to a new definition of national purpose. No great journalistic enterprise threw floodlights on the hidden crisis, treating it as more than a "story of the week."

SEVERAL PARAMEDICAL PRACTITIONERS made a stab at the troubled national condition. In 1979 Jimmy Carter, in his humorlessly intuitive way, briefly engaged the themes of retrenchment, disenchantment, and disillusion. The immediate business at hand was the energy squeeze; Carter was calling for "war footing" conservation and domestic effort to relieve American dependence on foreign oil. But he wanted to frame such policy broadly, and catch the troubled public imagination. Influenced by Lasch's *Culture of Narcissism,* Carter's pollster Pat Caddell sought to name the syndrome whereby Americans had (according to his surveys) turned profoundly pessimistic about their future, and the country's: *malaise.*

Lasch, a radical, argued a case that Caddell thought adaptable to Carter's centrist, post–New Deal outlook. Capitalism in its late-twentieth-century forms, Lasch wrote, "has evolved a new political ideology, welfare liberalism, which absolves individuals of moral responsibility and treats them as victims of social circumstance. . . . It has given rise to . . . the narcissistic culture of our time, which has translated the predatory individualism of the American Adam into a therapeutic jargon that celebrates not so much individualism as solipsism, justifying self-absorption as 'authenticity' and 'awareness.' "[9]

After an extraordinary ten-day retreat at Camp David communing with political leaders, scholars, and clergy, Carter "came down from the mountain" (as news accounts put it) and delivered a sermon on America's "crisis of confidence," a crisis striking "at the very heart and soul and spirit" of the nation, "threatening to destroy [our] social and . . . political fabric." Among a people who have "always believed in something called progress," said Carter, "too many of us now tend to worship self-indulgence and consumption." Noting that the "wounds are still very deep" from the "shocks and tragedy" of the 1960s and 1970s, acknowledging significant failings in his own performance as president and a specter of governmental "paralysis and stagnation and drift," Carter called on Americans to "face the truth" so we can "change our course. We simply must have faith in each other. Faith in our ability to govern ourselves and faith in the future of this nation. *Restoring that faith and that confidence to America is now the most important task we face*" (emphasis added).

But Dr. Carter had uttered the unspeakable, and his bedside manner didn't help. It would have taken an American de Gaulle, magisterially leading his nation to a recognition of postimperial realities, to speak as Carter tried to speak, and Carter was no de Gaulle. Journalist Hendrik Hertzberg, who wrote the "malaise" speech, likened the experience to bringing a plug to a highly charged socket and recoiling from the shock; there was something powerful there, but the wiring was off. The speech prompted such responses from leading Republicans as that "the crisis of confidence is of the President's own making" and his behavior "strange." A prominent Democrat said, "people don't want to be preached to, they want to be served."

And so, with that sense of misfire, the "malaise" speech for all its insight and daring, and much about the Carter presidency, got lodged in historical memory. Even before the Iranians' capture of American hostages later that year, a sense settled in of the American presidency as a shadow of its former self and our government as lately clueless, dysfunctional, choking on its own sprawl.[10]

A DECADE AND a half after Carter's speech, political scientist Michael J. Sandel picked up the theme and reexamined the elements of American malaise. In *Democracy's Discontent: America in Search of a New Public Philosophy,* he argued that the bigger government got in the twentieth century, the less it was trying to build a constituency that would sustain the logic of big government. Sandel wrote, "The nationalizing project that unfolded from the Progressive era to the New Deal to the Great Society . . . managed to create a strong national government but failed to cultivate a shared national identity. As the welfare state developed, it drew less on an ethic of social solidarity and mutual obligation and more on an ethic of fair procedures and individual rights. But the liberalism of the procedural republic proved an inadequate substitute for the strong sense of citizenship the welfare state requires."

Sandel argued, "As disillusion with government grew, politicians groped to articulate frustrations and discontents that the reigning political agenda did not capture." One political practitioner, the man who defeated Jimmy Carter for reelection, had a handle on, at least, the rhetoric of the situation.[11]

Ronald Reagan developed a masterful, uptown version of George Wallace's indictment of faceless Washington bureaucrats. "Those pluperfect hypocrites in Washington," Wallace would say, "I bet if you opened half of their briefcases, all you'd find would be a peanut butter sandwich." Rather than listen to common folk, they run the government according to the doctrines of "some pointy-headed pseudo-intellectual who can't even park his bicycle straight when he gets to the campus."[12]

Reagan focused resentment on the image of a monster — arrogant, sprawling, ineffective big government, and a manipulative, permanently dependent underclass taking advantage of it. "Reagan's attacks on the welfare queen in her Cadillac resounded," wrote a shrewd veteran of the Johnson White House, Harry McPherson. "Democrats," he argued, "might scoff about the insignificance of welfare costs, compared to the sums that Washington paid out to agribusiness each year. . . . Politically, there was no comparison. Everyone had a welfare-abuse story, observed or passed on; few people knew much about farm subsidies beyond an occasional stunning report in the papers which read like an account of Iran-Iraq casualties: awful, remote, soon forgotten."

Reagan's message rejected government as mindless and its wards as feckless; he prescribed self-reliance, optimism, and denial of the unpleasant: morning in America. The Democrats had no images as compelling as the "welfare queen." Hand-wringing about the "social safety net" sounded like so much of what Sandel called procedure.

Even earnest, straight-shooting Michael Dukakis — of all people — intuited Reagan's success as a kind of pop substitute for therapy. Asked at the start of the 1988 campaign why the most recent Democratic presidential contenders had fared so poorly, Dukakis paused and said, "Fritz [Mondale] didn't come across as an optimist, someone who could lift people."[13]

DESPITE ALL THAT'S to be said and documented about Hollywood's commercialism, some of the major studios, along with small, independent filmmakers, addressed the themes of American loss more consistently and profoundly than did political leaders or journalists. Hollywood had always seen crime, drugs, and the meanness of streets as good film material. But in the 1970s and 1980s it took up the effects of the lost war in Vietnam on veterans and their families in *The Deer Hunter* (1978), *Coming Home* (1978), and *Born on the Fourth of July* (1989). It looked at the unraveling of American agricultural life in *Country* (1984) and a scenario for environmental disaster in *The China Syndrome* (1979). *Norma Rae* (1979), an old-fashioned tale of discontent on the assembly line, and *Roger & Me* (1989), a low-budget independent documentary about the CEO of General Motors, caught the widening gap between management and the industrial workforce. *Silkwood* (1983) and *Wall Street* (1987) examined managerial greed in still more sinister light.

What the mainstream press picked up on as to displacement in American life coming out of the 1960s and early 1970s was the celebration of escapism and withdrawal. But these were on the whole passing or side-shot critiques (like Tom Wolfe's witty contribution, "the 'Me' Decade") rather than active engagement.

Active engagement was the province of those who saw the trend toward escapism as a case of commercial opportunity knocking. Escapism and the cross-breeding entertainment and communications industries fueled each other, yielding in due course entities like Time Warner and a Disney encompassing Capital Cities/ABC, aspiring masters of an infotainment universe. If the frenzied merging, acquiring, leveraging, trading, marketing of the 1980s was a meager imitation of the boom times of earlier eras, and on a narrow social scale, it nevertheless fed a cult of consumption beckoning all to the universal shopping mall.

Social withdrawal was not only an attitude but a behavioral option, thanks to devices like the Walkman (which helped prompt a suggestive sociological term, cocooning), video games, VCRs, and the Internet. It was possible to remove oneself from the surrounding environment and create a private, controlled one filled with "virtual" associations and interaction.

The journalistic and film handles on these mood and behavior patterns echoed as mantras for the times: from the activism, hedonism, and revolutionary heat of the 1960s to *The Big Chill, Wall Street,* "the 'Me' Generation," the time of the "yuppie." From preoccupation with blasting establishment structures to preoccupation with self, pop therapy, money, trendiness, the acquisition of gadgetry.

Numbers helped shape the mood, as well as tell the story. Turnout in presidential elections topped 60 percent of the voting population through the 1950s and 1960s. In 1972 turnout fell to 55.2 percent, matching that level once (in 1992) but in every other presidential election since then falling well below it. (In 1996 it was 49.7 percent.)

What was true nationally was more pronounced at the local level. In the same time frame, congressional and gubernatorial election turnout in non-presidential-election years fell from percentages in the 40s, where it had held steady for decades, to its current level in the 30s — from 46.6 percent of the voting-age population in 1970 to under 40 percent through the 1980s and 1990s.[14]

As to who was finding out about what, 1973 was a peak year for the number of daily newspapers in the country (1,774) and total daily circulation for them (63.1 million); both have fallen more or less steadily since. By 1998 the number of daily newspapers in the United States stood at 1,489, and their combined circulation was down to 56.2 million. Average daily newspaper readership, almost 80 percent of the population in the mid-1960s, stayed at that level into the early 1970s. Then it went into free fall, dropping about a percentage point or half-point a year. By 1998 average daily readership was down to

57.9 percent of the total population. A close-in look revealed the deepening pattern of occasional reading: the habit of picking up the paper a few days a week, but with declining frequency.[15]

The newsmagazines, which owed their franchise to the shortage of strong national and foreign reporting in the bygone era in which they were founded, struggled for a place in the crowded "communications revolution" marketplace. Gradually they began to trade in their position in hard news for the vagaries of health tips, leisure "trends," and entertainment celebrities.[16]

Television was the beneficiary of print news media's distress by some measures, but the ratings for television news were further proof of the public's inclinations. CBS's and NBC's news ratings — the percentage of all households watching the news — fell from 14.5 percent and 13 percent, respectively, in 1970–71 to 7.8 percent (CBS) and 8.4 percent (NBC) in 1998. ABC News, which had a 7.7 percent rating with weak programming in 1970, competed more hotly with CBS and NBC thereafter before joining the slide; its 1998 rating was 8 percent.[17]

Richard Ford evokes the mood these numbers suggest in his novel *Independence Day*, set in 1988. Ford's hero Frank Bascombe, a former sportswriter turned suburban New Jersey real estate broker, speaks wanly of his post-divorce "Existence Period" and observes:

> falling property values now ride through the trees like an odorless, colorless mist settling through the still air where all breathe it in, all sense it, though our new amenities — the new police cruisers, the new crosswalks . . . do what they civically can to ease our minds off worrying, convince us our worries aren't worries, or at least not ours alone but everyone's — no one's — and that staying the course, holding the line, riding the cyclical nature of things are what this country's all about, and thinking otherwise is to drive optimism into retreat, to be paranoid and in need of expensive 'treatment' out of state.[18]

IT'S POSSIBLE, and instructive, to posit that what American society was passing through was a profound, buried depression — of the psychological and emotional rather than the economic kind —

together with mankind's best friends among defense mechanisms against depression: denial and escapism.

For the accumulation of loss, disillusionment, embarrassment, and dashed dreams that Americans suffered collectively in the 1960s and 1970s had to trigger effects more profound than falling ratings for news and rising ones for entertainment, "cocooning," and yuppie culture. Those were merely symptoms.[19]

PART 2

Disarray

FOUR

Structure

BENEATH THE COUNTRY'S outward reversals and unfocused perception of them, adding to the syndrome of depression and denial, fundamental structural elements of American politics had disintegrated. This was less a heralded event than a creeping change in the weather. The country had experienced sorely divided government many times, with presidents, Congress, or the Supreme Court stalemating one another. But by the 1970s, growing bloated in dimension and numbers, American governance was passing from merely divided to gridlocked and dysfunctional; from Walter Lippmann's vision of mastery to his warning of drift.[1]

Contributing to governmental atrophy were factors as old as the republic, sometimes bound up with traumatic new ones. In the early 1990s, for example, the surgeon general of the United States and the *Journal of the American Medical Association* called for stringent gun controls on the basis of rising rates of urban gunshot wounds and deaths. The figures, according to the journal, were evidence of a public health epidemic. Here was a prime symptom of urban social breakdown. But the odds against legislating meaningful gun control in this country were not only a function of the influence of the gun lobby. They also flowed back to such root facts as the equal weight of wild and rural states in the U.S. Senate to densely urbanized ones (unimaginable to the founding fathers who double-locked equal Senate representation for each state into the Constitution).[2]

Then too the nation's political parties, which for a hundred and fifty years were the vehicles for public participation in politics and government and communication channels in the bargain, were by the 1980s effectively out of the business they'd been in. "Once the central guiding forces in American electoral behavior, the parties are now perceived with almost complete indifference by a large proportion of the public," wrote one scholar. The sense that "at a policy level no party . . . could offer solutions that 'worked' over the long haul" fed a "growing disenchantment" with politics, added another. "When parties are absent or . . . have become Cheshire cats of which very little is left but the smile, pathologies multiply," observed a third. "No parties at all leaves a society out of reach, out of control, and no modernized regime can afford, in the long run, to settle on this unsafe and unproductive solution," warned a fourth.[3]

America's parties had connected towns and cities to state capitals, and the country to Washington. They'd assisted the press in maintaining the relevance of "the news" to the reader and viewer, whether the struggles reported were between parties at election time or waged within them between South and North, East and West, reformers and bosses. The parties and their splits and feuds, their conventions and campaigns, had helped hold the larger national drama together for politicians, press, and audience.[4]

The parties performed other functions crucial to the workings of public life, functions also now vanished. They'd groomed and vetted candidates for office. Many of course were hacks, but others, from Andrew Jackson to the Roosevelts to the La Follettes to Hubert Humphrey, founded state and national party lineages of distinction that lasted for generations.

And the parties served as vehicles for building broad coalition-based majorities as catalysts for the conversion of single-issue advocacy into practical, concerted action. They carried a weight that meant that politics was not simply a function of personality or "character." The spectacle of a serious political figure like Robert Dole in 1996 rendered absurd in his effort to appeal to both centrists and New Right extremists was a sign of how times had changed since the parties, by coalescing interests, helped bear the burden of a campaign, relieving the candidate from having to fly it solo.[5]

Thus the parties reflected the threads of the social and economic fabric of the country as they were. Where there was exclusion at the top there was also, in the New Deal and postwar years, more and more flexing of political muscle on the part of ethnic minorities, and later of blacks and women. The arrangements the parties brokered at the local level in matters of schools and roads and taxes, in the caucuses that chose candidates and picked delegates to state and national conventions, were integral to the workings of communities and to their interactions on up the ladders of governance. In the New York City neighborhoods and Connecticut towns where I grew up in the 1940s and 1950s, that was part of the way people lived, identified themselves, and associated with one another, across class, ethnic, and color lines — linked by party participation.

POLITICAL SCIENTISTS DISTINGUISH "parties in government" and "parties as organizations" — numerically minuscule collections of officials and apparatchiks — from the tens of millions of people who, in theory, constitute the "parties in the electorate." The former live on as skeletons: as instruments of an all-too-hollow control of public office and management of elections, as hitching posts for political action committees (PACs) in the high-price influence game. As such, they bear small relation to what they were when, integrally linked to parties in the electorate, they were the machinery of political coalition, bargaining, and action that used to function at national, state, and local levels.

Those mechanisms engaged not merely lobbyists and the agents of what has been called the "bastard feudal" network of campaign consultants. They were parties in the business of legislating and governing first and foremost. They were partisan vehicles for shrill, ideological name-calling — the modern model — a far distant second. And they involved average citizens who thought of themselves as "grass-roots" Democrats and Republicans, showed up at caucuses and campaign rallies, volunteered to assist their parties' candidates in election season, paid attention to their words and actions.[6]

A factor in the decline of the modern parties in the electorate was of course the middle-class revolution of the New Deal, wartime, and postwar years. That part of the Democratic Party's prowess which derived in the mid–twentieth century from the allegiance of urban working-class voters, and from the clout of the large unions, eroded in pace with the "up and out" movement of blue-collar workers to white-collar jobs and incomes, and to suburban neighborhoods.

Postwar demographics made room for a loosening of Republican Party identity, too. A broader, more fluid middle-class America meant a bigger, more unpredictable floating vote.

Then too the coalition-oriented, broadly communal aspects of party identification that attracted the participation of past generations of Americans were precisely those that 1960s and 1970s radicals inclined against. The turnoff deepened as prevailing attitudes evolved from protest and activism to disaffection and preoccupation with self and material things.[7]

The more immediate, widely discussed reasons for the erosion of the "parties in the electorate" were the emergence of television in the 1960s as the principal vehicle for political discourse and news, and the post-1968, post-Watergate party reforms. Soon the two were working in tandem. For the reforms — which included the proliferation of presidential primaries from a strategic few to a glut of them across the nation, "the permanent campaign," as Sidney Blumenthal dubbed it — effectively handed what was left of the party bosses' grip on politics to television. And television turned politics in the direction of its own essence: visual entertainment.[8]

Television, wrote Ronald Reagan's pollster Richard Wirthlin, "completely altered . . . the way candidates communicate with the electorate." Add the computer to the mix, he continued, "and the way candidates conceive and implement their campaigns" was transformed "through the guiding hand of the pollster and the strategist armed with the analytical and statistical tools."[9]

But that wasn't all. Once again, deterministic forces converged with freely made choices. In the 1970s, the same time frame that television and the computer upended the mechanics of politics, Congress in the name of reform (through the federal election campaign legislation of 1971 and 1974) and the Supreme Court (refining that legislation in its 1976 *Buckley v. Valeo* decision) blundered their way to a new set of rules, displacing the old party scheme of things. By the 1980s, the result was law-of-the-jungle rapacity in two parts: a campaign finance system that effectively sanctified the deployment of political money as free speech, and a Congress dependent on special-interest political action committees as their middlemen for that money. This was not exactly what the congressional and party reformers of the late 1960s and early 1970s had in mind.[10]

Fittingly for an era that saw the revival of the cult of the market, politics by the 1990s boiled down to raising vast sums of money to buy television advertising. What did that mean in fact?

Television, for its part, has become at once so smotheringly ubiquitous, so amorphous and ephemeral, that it's easy to overemphasize its influence. "Current preoccupation with the media," argued Michael Schudson, "mistakes the public parlor of loquaciousness for the heart of society." But television did displace newspaper reading. And as Robert Putnam has noted, studies show that "TV viewing is strongly and negatively related to social trust and group membership, whereas the same correlations with newspaper reading are positive."[11]

And television did fill the procedural vacuum in politics that opened up with the demise of the bosses, machines, and conventions of old-style campaigning. "The image transmitted by TV and the other media is of a person, not the abstraction known as a political party," noted one scholar. Thus, added another, "it is candidates rather than parties that are now viewed as being responsible for solving, or failing to solve, our current political problems," pushing politics ever more from matters of substance to matters of personality.

In Neil Postman's description of the trivializing effect of such personalization in the 1984 presidential campaign debates, Ronald Reagan and Walter Mondale

> were less concerned with giving arguments than with "giving off" impressions, which is what television does best. Post-debate commentary largely avoided any evaluation of the candidates' ideas, since there were none to evaluate. Instead, the debates were conceived as boxing matches, the relevant question being, Who KO'd whom? The answer was determined by the "style" of the men — how they looked, fixed their gaze, smiled, and delivered one-liners. In the second debate, President Reagan got off a swell one-liner when asked a question about his age. The following day, several newspapers indicated that Ron had KO'd Fritz with his joke.[12]

V. John Tunney, with little to offer beyond telegenic looks and the name of his father (a great boxing champion), was an example of how in a time of weakening party structure a candidate could leap straight into high elective office (in his case, a single undistinguished term as a U.S. senator from California in the 1970s). Unlike multimillionaires Averell Harriman and Nelson Rockefeller, who acquired the governorship of New York in succession through bargains with the state Democratic and Republican parties, modern aspirants to high office of great wealth like Steve Forbes and the here-today, gone-tomorrow California candidates Michael Huffington and Al Cecchi threw their millions on the airwaves — literally, into the air.

Martin P. Wattenberg, in 1984, wrote that as early as 1950 scholars in the field had agreed that if the parties began to lose their effectiveness, "voter frustration might set in motion more extreme tendencies of both the left and the right. . . . This fear has been at least partially realized. . . . Parties once channeled political conflict and kept policy differences within reasonable bounds. . . . With parties increasingly less able to resolve these conflicts, the tone of American politics is becoming more negative and bitter." The new political free-fire zone was ripe territory for the "wedge" campaigns at which the New Right proved so adept. The idea was to mobilize adherents of single or narrow interests — anti-abortion, anti–gun control — to turn out for primaries and secure nominations for extremist candidates like Representatives Helen Chenoweth of Idaho and Steve Stockman of Texas, as far from the mainstreams of what remained of the parties as they could get.[13]

Politicians of a certain age found the terrain they'd known when they entered politics — a network of insurgent and established organized representation of labor, business, agriculture, and ethnic minorities — vanishing. In its place was an anonymous, atomized wasteland; the essential points of connection were its television sets. Add to the new politics, observed former governor of Texas Ann Richards in the wake of her defeat for a second term in 1994, the tendency for the press "to value (or communicate) all opinions equally. The talking head of the moment considers anyone willing to put quotes around their utterances as worthy of presentation as 'the other side.' There was a time when the word 'crackpot' meant something—but no longer. The effect on the voting public divides and isolates rather than creating an atmosphere in which common interests can coalesce."[14]

For the hungry candidate starting out, the idea was no longer to work your way up the ladder of a rooted political organization, or fight to reform it, or demonstrate an ability to build a coalition. The trick instead for the ambitious entrant to the game was to buy into the ranks of the new political consultant mercenaries, armed with state-of-the-art "media campaign" firepower, selling, as one of them put it, "magic." How were the voters to make choices? By watching and listening to the fruits of the mercenaries' skill at merchandising an image, a vague theme or single-issue refrain, and, more and more, to their deadly techniques for driving up opponents' "negatives." In place of the old political structure was an electronic arena for free agents and their handlers; a market model driven by money, television entertainment values, and the power of negative advertising.

Name-calling was nothing new in politics; its use to the exclusion of all other political discourse was. As *The New York Times* put it in a headline at the end of the 1998 congressional election season, "From Sea to Shining Sea, the TV Campaign Is All Attack Ads, All the Time."[15]

ONCE AGAIN, HOLLYWOOD was quick to note the new lock between campaigning and television. *The Candidate* featured Robert Redford as a telegenic, accidental politician (modeled on John Tunney) who gets lucky. Redford's curtain line following his election ("What do we do now?") became shorthand for the media-age "politician lite."

Less remarked upon was the full effect of television's growing dominance over newspapers in its role as shaping force in political culture and discourse. Television is not only predominantly an entertainment medium but one regulated by government. It is therefore institutionally weaker out of the gate than newspapers. There are no landmark First Amendment cases on the order of *Times v. Sullivan* or the Pentagon Papers decision involving television news (unless you count *Herbert v. Lando,* a case arising from CBS's *60 Minutes* program, in which the news media lost major First Amendment ground).[16]

Chief among the imperatives of the visual image are compression, fast-cutting, the breakup of linear continuity, all to avoid boredom. But the imperatives risk incoherence. That is why, having spawned the quick-hit sound bite, television news makes such a point of reaching for continuity when it's available, with melodramatic graphics on the order of "America Held Hostage: Day 189" during the Iran crisis of 1979–81. During the Bush administration, NBC News ran story after story slugged "The War on Drugs," echoing official rhetoric and featuring official film footage of military aircraft and ships prowling for narcotics smugglers. Here was tense film plus cops and robbers plus narrative line — lacking only a journalistic or governmental resolution beyond the rhetoric and the images.[17]

Television's standout moment as an adversary watchdog is, as it has been for almost half a century, Edward R. Murrow's 1954 CBS News program calling Senator Joseph McCarthy to account. Long before the end of the century the unspoken rule in the ever more second-guessed, anxious world of television news was, in the distinguished former network news reporters Marvin and Bernard Kalb's words, "Get it first, but first get it second" — that is, beat the other networks if you can, but don't get out in front of the newspapers; it's not safe out there.[18]

Murrow took on McCarthy effectively in an analytic format. He showed film of the senator flinging around his charges and innuendoes, and then detailed the exaggerations and distortions. Television newsmen today, operating in talk-show formats, are susceptible to being outgunned by well-programmed political performers; once the political and career government professions digested fully the lessons of press power arrayed against them in the Vietnam and Watergate years, they were primed to turn the tables. George Bush's "macho" besting of Dan Rather in their live confrontation in 1988 over the Iran-Contra scandal, like the Reagan White House's mastery of the "media event," reflected shrewd attendance to the disasters that had befallen their predecessors when they lost control of their agendas, political standing — and televised images.

Another sign of the times was the media stratagem of bypassing the news altogether. Bill Clinton's campaign managers in 1992 — worried about reporters' probes into the governor's draft evasion, marijuana use, and more recent philandering — discovered that (as one of them, Mandy Grunwald, put it) "the more [people] see him, the more they like him — which isn't true" of George Bush and Ross Perot. From there it was a quick call to schedule Clinton into entertainment formats like *The Arsenio Hall Show*. There, the topics of interest to persistent reporters could be kept at bay, and there the made-for-video Clinton could score.[19]

NEWSPAPERS COULD UNCOVER and track stories like Vietnam and Watergate through mud and detour and canceled check and dry hole, detail by detail. Television could not, but it could do something else. As the Vietnam War ground to an opaque end in 1975, *New Yorker* television critic Michael J. Arlen wrote that, "with its parade of surreal or superficial stories" about the war, its "pictographs" and "icon[s] of an airplane or a gun firing . . . [or] of a bleeding child," its "disconnected visual glimpses or isolated snatches of dialogue, as if from some massive ongoing novel, whose core the novelist has somehow omitted," television was ubiquitous in "covering" Vietnam, while missing the meanings of the story. In so doing, he concluded, television network news "contribute[d] to the unreality, and thus the dysfunction of American life."[20]

Much ink has been spilled by social scientists in debating — in a vacuum — the question whether television coverage of the Vietnam War "caused" the erosion of public support for the war. The real issue is considerably larger, more complex, and other. Arlen was way ahead of the social scientists in discerning it in its nuance: the relation of television and entertainment culture to contemporary alienation.[21]

According to postmodern laws of diminishing returns, disturbing, even wretched excess was required in order to achieve public attention or response; thus the dentist's-drill whine of the political ads. And thus (in Sissela Bok's words) "the mass marketing of violence as sexy and sexuality as violent" in film and television "entertainment."[22]

In his 1997 novel *Underworld,* Don DeLillo captured the darker side of television's power, the electronic potential for taking film-noir effect to total nihilism, in a motif about "the Texas Highway Killer" videotape. His device is a fictional amalgam of haunting film phenomena like the videotaped beating of Rodney King by the Los Angeles police and the Zapruder tape of the assassination of President Kennedy. In *Underworld,* viewers watch obsessively the network television replays of footage of a serial killer's murder of a stranger on a high-speed freeway. (At times the killer, on the loose, calls in to a news anchor, deadpan, to comment.) On the tape, the killer's car pulls into pace with the victim's. The killer fires and then fades back. The whole scene is filmed by the victim's young daughter, idling the highway hours away with the family's new toy. DeLillo writes,

> And there is something about videotape, isn't there, and this particular kind of serial crime? . . . You sit there and wonder if this kind of crime became more possible when the means of taping an event and playing it immediately, without a neutral interval, a balancing space and time, became widely available. Taping-and-playing intensifies and compresses the event. It dangles a need to do it again. You sit there thinking that the serial murder has found its medium, or vice versa — an act of shadow technology, of compressed time and repeated images, stark and glary and unremarkable. . . . You don't want [your wife] to give you any crap about it's on all the time, they show it a thousand times a day. They show it because it exists, because they have to show it, because this is why they're out there, to provide our entertainment.
>
> The more you watch the tape, the deader and colder and more relentless it becomes. The tape sucks the air right out of your chest but you watch it every time.[23]

THE POLITICAL GAME became the fitting of political purpose to television's forms. Successful politics increasingly demanded telegenic presence, of course; fluency in the patter of the sound bite, deftness at the nasty insinuation of political advertising, mastery of post-game spin. But also adaptation to television's dreamy, half-attentive blurs, Arlen's "parade" of the surreal and superficial, De-

Lillo's compression of the horrific into the unremarkable, the "pictographs" packing visual impact and disconnected, if any, meaning.

And because what had been a political-party game had metamorphosed into a media game, the press was complicit in it. Its role became more front and center, and more awkward and ambiguous, than in the past. Noble "watchdog"? Or marketing-minded player of a media game parallel to that of the politicians and their handlers, concerned, bottom-line, with ratings?

The masters of the political media game noted (with pleasure) this new problem for the press early on. Roger Ailes, protagonist of Joe McGinnis's *The Selling of the President* and orchestrator of the 1988 Bush campaign's alarming Willie Horton ad: "Look at trash TV, look at the lines blurring between tabloid journalism and television. I would submit that the political campaigns are among the cleanest things on television today." The late Republican National Committee chairman Lee Atwater, in 1990, shortly before he became ill: "If you want to look at a solid trend for the last 15 to 20 years, it is that the American people are cynical and turned off about all institutions, and politics is only one of them. Bull permeates everything. In other words, . . . the American people think politics and politicians, . . . media and journalists, . . . big business, big labor, [are] full of baloney."[24]

The press compounded the problem at every turn, and the imperatives imposed by television's forms helped. In stepping into their new "media game" roles, reporters evolved from stereotypically cool, detached witnesses into attention-getting "personalities," a role formerly reserved for oddball showman columnists like Walter Winchell and Drew Pearson, operators on the journalistic fringe.

The loudmouths of the Sunday morning political talk shows, the inquisitors of the presidential press conferences, the pious schoolmasters of the presidential debate panels, the smug instant analysts of the post-speech or debate wrap-ups — these were the identities people were learning to attach to the peers and craftsmen of the press.[25]

FINALLY, THE DECLINE of political and governmental efficacy meant that what was playing out — on television — was more horror show or charade than a reality with which one could engage, or move forward with in time. Televised images of the Democrats' national convention at Chicago in 1968 amounted to an apocalypse for their party. The medium's long vigil over Watergate was that for Republicans. To be sure, Henry Kissinger helped Richard Nixon to a personalized, televised set of diplomatic coups in Russia and China, but these failed to ease the American debacle in Vietnam or to translate into political insurance for a government sinking under scandal.

Instead, the continuing sequence of presidents undone — Johnson, Nixon, Ford, Carter — with their accompanying spectacles of disaster (an unpopular and unwinnable war, riots in the street, trade deficits, raging inflation, the oil cartel's diktat, "America held hostage") signaled problems out of control, government breaking down. So did George Wallace and Ronald Reagan with their venom directed at governmental folly and bloat. So did the new tableau of ungovernability in Washington.

The city where statesmen once guided the United States to twentieth-century world leadership and social justice became the domain of tribes of expensive lobbyists. In the 1880s senators and congressmen themselves had frankly represented industrial interests. A century later they and their aides served in office long enough to establish entrée, then glided across town to lobby for corporate America, trade associations, and other interests.

PACs became the financial underpinning of the relationship between officeholders and lawyer-lobbyists. The lobbying firms borrowed from direct marketing technology, buttressing their practice of persuasion behind closed doors with the ability to mount strident, bogus "grass-roots" letter-writing and phone campaigns. By these means the lobbyists helped fill the functional space vacated by the parties — at a price to their clients, and at the cost of mounting public disgust with Washington and its ways.[26]

The result — "partisan" vitriol at the national level, alienation from parties and public affairs down the line — emptied politics of meaning for millions of Americans. "If you think about it, the foundation, the heart, the fabric of democracy is motivated, interested, participating citizens, and we're eating away at that in the way [politics today] rolls out," remarked House minority leader Richard Gephardt in 1998.[27]

Alone among the sequence of late-twentieth-century American presidents, Reagan fashioned a way to make alienation from politics and government work for him. Reagan's contrarian stance toward a government in ill repute and his benign, dreamy mode of operation were a happy mix. His masterpiece was his regime of tax cuts, underscoring the proposition that government had become irrelevant and counterproductive. But Reagan's success was in great part personal, and a matter of timing. His was a triumph by a veteran of entertainment culture just as the latter was colonizing political culture. It was an exception to the late-night talk show rule that American politics and government had become a bad joke.

By the late 1990s, the combination of structural decay in American governance and politics and populist nihilism about both hung over the country like a toxic cloud. "It's a time [in] which big ideas failed," said one pollster. Filling such space, the forms of modern politics — preeminent among them the snarling derision of ad hominem television advertising — were designed to mobilize grievance over a period of weeks, but had the effect of instilling disgust over a period of years. "The most notable thing to me," campaign consultant Raymond D. Strother remarked in 1998, "is how difficult it is this year to penetrate the public mind, how cynical they are and how . . . skeptical of anything anybody says. . . . Negative advertising still works, but it works less well than it once did. It's just the abundance of it. People have built up an immunity or resistance to it."[28]

FOR AN EXTENDED, euphoric period, a booming stock market, low inflation, and record employment figures eased distress. But those bright tidings conflicted with longer term, more systemic dark ones as the decade wound down: about the corporate downsizing that helped fuel the booming stock market, about sluggish and slipping economic productivity, about the marginal nature of many jobs touted as "new," about a widening gap between the very poor and the very rich, and between job opportunities for those with college educations and those lacking them; about Americans' loss of trust in one another and in the nation's course.[29]

The boom years were "not likely to recreate the postwar sense of bounty," wrote Louis Uchitelle of *The New York Times* in 1997.

"Instead, people are carrying into the future the residue of the stagnant years, and their compromised expectations. . . . Holding onto a job now takes precedence over upward mobility, or getting decent annual raises. . . . Longer hours on the job have displaced the pre-1973 goal of more leisure time." Those in the business of seeking credit for boom times celebrated the creation of new jobs replacing downsized ones. The follow-up reports and the fine print made plain that many were at lower wages, carrying less security, than the jobs lost.[30]

Reports on the campaign to push welfare dependents into jobs were disappointing. The rhetoric of "workfare" was proving to bear little relation to the costs and difficulties of moving people immersed for decades in the culture of welfare up and out of it. Members of the soaring "temp" and "permatemp" workforce, statistics in officials' claims for economic expansion, found jobs but meager, if any, benefit protection or employment security. At the other end of the workforce, the news was of middle managers downsized out of corporate structures in the early '90s, struggling "with what is, not what used to be" at decade's end. *The Wall Street Journal,* no prophet of doom, quoted management experts who cited "new data show[ing] a 'pretty sharp decline' in long-term job retention among the most-tenured workers."[31]

In between, the middle class was economically stalled, compared with increases in net gain for those at the upper end of the ladder, and those at the very bottom benefiting from government entitlements, subsidies, and training programs. "The wages of people with only four years of college are no longer rising," *The New York Times* reported in 1998, and people in the middle "are much more on their own than lower-income workers."[32]

Along with the obsession with lotteries and legalized gambling spreading across the country since the 1970s — Americans bet *$638 billion* in 1997, almost triple the figure ten years earlier, and lost more than $50 billion of that — came symptoms of associated social ills. One was a boom in compulsive gambling, with quantifiable costs in fraud, embezzlement, prosecution, and jail terms. More serious was the hold of the lottery's "luck ethic" on the poor, "who see gambling as an investment, not a form of entertainment," according to Robert Goodman, who studied the phenomenon for the Ford Foundation. The Powerball lottery craze in a cluster of participating states in the summer of 1998, featuring frenzied travel across state lines to gain access to it and long lines of purchasers waving big bills to buy tickets in bulk, was a sign that for millions of Americans the luck ethic overshadowed the work ethic — even in boom times.[33]

In 1997, with the economy in high gear and stock market prices soaring to record levels, the Pew Research Center for the People and the Press reported that "Americans' optimism about their own present and future . . . [is] at near record levels." In boom times, that was the good news. Yet respondents "rate[d] the state of the nation today nearly as low as in bad economic times or when political scandal soured the public mood," as at the depths of the Watergate era. Citing concerns about "seemingly intractable moral and social problems," crime, entitlement programs, deficits, and partisanship, the survey found the distance "between optimism about personal future and the country's future unprecedented."[34]

Press reports of such negative indicators were food for thought, but isolated. As with the newsmagazines' "running out of everything" cover stories in the 1970s, they came and went. They led to nothing politically or in journalistic follow-through to compare with the effect of early-twentieth-century journalistic muckraking on the subjects of working and living conditions of the poor or the arrogance and greed of the "robber barons" of that era. Furthermore, as we shall see, news business executives had decided this was not the kind of journalism they wanted.

And in any event there was bread, and there were circuses; entertainment everywhere, on proliferating cable television channels, in Blockbuster video rental stores, in "cineplex" movie complexes, on the World Wide Web. Enthusiasts of the on-line age were boundless in their excitement about the Internet as a boon for managing one's life, for exploration, for joining electronic communities, for trading your identity in for a frisky or adventurous new one in a cyberspace MUD ("multi-user dungeon," or on-line virtual community).

Then came hints of a downside: research suggesting correlations between time devoted to the Internet and increases in levels of depression and loneliness. Even a cyberculture booster like Sherry Turkle of MIT began to worry about the social and psychological implications of "virtual rape" and "virtual murder." A Columbia graduate student went to jail for fifteen years for taking an on-line game of seduction and torture from the computer room to the bedroom. Two suburban teenagers addicted to violent video games patterned on combat "conditioning" techniques devised by U.S. military trainers murdered fourteen classmates and a teacher.[35]

The tics were reminiscent of Scott Fitzgerald's description of the late 1920s when, with the stock market still booming, contemporaries began to fall " 'accidentally' . . . and purposely" from skyscrapers, and "a widespread neurosis began to be evident, faintly signalled, like a nervous beating of the feet, by the popularity of cross-word puzzles."[36]

UNLIKE OTHER ENTERPRISING journalism of its sort, a 1996 *Washington Post* series, "The Politics of Mistrust," took a passing look at political party affiliation. Tying "a collapse of trust in human nature" on the part of most Americans to "an erosion of trust in government and virtually every other institution," the study found only one in four Americans saying they "trusted the federal government all or most of the time," compared with three in four in 1964. Wrote *Post* reporter Thomas Edsall,

> The glue that held together the core constituencies of the traditional Democratic coalition — blue-collar workers and union members, blacks, urban political machines based in working class neighborhoods — was . . . a sense of unity in the face of a Republican adversary aligned with business and corporate management. Those traditional divisions are collapsing. . . . the electorate is breaking up into increasingly complex units in which fundamental characteristics of one's identity — sex, marital status, depth of religious conviction, race — are shaping partisan allegiance.[37]

Edsall, deeply interested in the societal basis of politics, was an anomaly among political reporters. Elsewhere, the press treated the widespread disaffection in passing, sometimes with irony (for example, "Whatever Happened to Politics?" a *New York Times Magazine* package of three slight think-pieces about the distractions and anomie of the late 1990s). But in general, the press passed over the significance of the disappearance of political parties as a force in sustaining citizens' interest in local and national public life.

All the reports duly noted, along with appalling public ignorance of the most basic aspects of politics and government in the much heralded "information age," a generalized disgust for partisanship (as in shrill catfights between Democrats and Republicans in Washington). The very *idea* of political parties themselves as a meaningful, effective presence in people's consciousness or communities, of the vital structural role they'd long played in American life, was missing in action.[38]

FIVE

Character

AS NATURE ABHORS a vacuum, a natural effect of the disintegration of governance and the parties, and metamorphosis of politics into a media game, was the mounting obsession in the 1980s with the private lives of prominent politicians and other public figures. For the press and the public alike, this obsession with the personal helped fill the space once taken up by lively engagement with the issue-oriented and procedural aspects of politics and government.

The press tried gamely to play by the old rules, largely ignoring the structural origins of the new fixation on the private and personal. It worked at mustering skepticism in the face of rumors. It worried about boundaries of privacy. But the new political landscape was treacherous. Reporters had trouble avoiding being cast as agents in a campaign's guerrilla attacks on an opponent, featuring damaging clips of film and tape. The news cycle (which used to rest overnight) operated nonstop, thanks to such innovations as twenty-four-hour cable news, round-the-clock campaign polling techniques, and the Internet. In its efforts to be competitive in this anarchic environment, the press sometimes resembled a trained athlete in a match gone mad. What the press did achieve in such coverage, adding to a growing confusion, was a furious backlash against itself.

In the press's favor for decades had been the public's half-appreciation of the dual nature of the journalistic mission: first, as just-the-facts reporter; second, as investigative watchdog whose reportage has real-world consequences. Thus, surveys since the mid-1980s have recorded ratings well above 50 percent (sometimes approaching 70 percent) for press scrutiny of political leaders as "worth it because it keeps [them] from doing things that should not be done," and against it by comparable margins for excessive intrusiveness. Typically, a *New York Times*/CBS poll in 1992 found that "55 percent of registered voters nationwide said the press went too far in disclosing details of Presidential candidates' private lives, but 50 percent said that nothing reported in the current campaign should not have been reported." In fact, such seeming contradictions fairly reflected public ambivalence, as distinct from hostility, toward the press.[1]

Nevertheless by the early 1990s, the press in its watchdog role was seen to have turned increasingly rabid. Journalistic method in a feeding frenzy, wrote Larry Sabato, is "a repetitive, disproportionate stress on scandal, a 'more of the same' theme, a 'what can you expect from politicians' tone that deepens, extends, and reinforces the enduring public suspicion of all things political." With rather more acid, Suzanne Garment argued that reporters writing about women exposed in liaisons with politicians display a "cynicism toward the woman in one of those scandals . . . matched by the contempt some of the more thoughtful of them have for their own role in the process, for they are no more innocent than she is. They know they are not simply doing the solemn job of revealing the character traits of national politicians but [are instead] acting as integral cogs in the sensationalist scandal machine."[2]

But the press was by no means solely responsible for excessive, invasive coverage of political figures. Indeed, the topic prompted a riddlesome name for itself that, as to blame, passed the buck: "the character issue."

The character issue made everyone hot under the collar: officials, candidates and their apparatchiks, political scientists and other scholars who study the field, journalists critical of their profession and, in return, journalists who saw themselves condemned for doing their duty, and the sophisticated and the unsophisticated among the audience.

It also rendered elite, high-end news organizations and the most salacious tabloid ones sisters under their skins. For journalistic traffic in character, unlike reports of visits to earth from space aliens, was common to both. The important difference between the performance of *The New York Times* and *The Washington Post* and that of the sleazy supermarket tabloids was the high degree of internal debate and ambivalence on the part of mainstream news organizations in heading into the traffic. That ambivalence expressed itself publicly, in a spirit of self-therapy or atonement, in the occasional soul-searching news analysis or editorial about the dubious merits of coverage of public figures' private lives. Thus, in the wake of one such wave of revelation, a press report quoted leading journalistic spokesmen in stalwart defense of the First Amendment ("You cannot edit in fear of what a court might do" — Michael Gartner, then head of NBC News) in conflict with those who feared for its future ("My visceral reaction was that this is the kind of thing that's going to get us regulated" — Jane E. Kirtley, executive director of the Reporters Committee for Freedom of the Press).[3]

The phenomenon of the character issue is a microcosm of the contemporary journalistic dilemma. So let us take a step back and pause on its emergence and evolution.

IN THE MEDIA stone age, the great men of government and the great men of the Washington press corps did business about the great issues of the day in an atmosphere of great trust. With the rarest of exceptions, that atmosphere precluded press concern with public officials' susceptibility to alcohol or libido. Joseph Alsop, grandee of the ancien régime, observed in his memoirs, "Having people in power at your table is important and useful for two basic reasons. In the first place, one might get *a line on the character* of a person in power by seeing him or her informally at the dinner table. Second, especially if he or she sees you at your own dinner table, the official may get a line on what kind of person you may be and can decide, on the basis of this, whether you are trustworthy. This, in turn, lays a foundation for the right business relationship between the reporter and the man in power" (emphasis added).[4]

Alsop describes a socially ordered environment for doing "business," as well as the place of "character" within it. Let us count the ways in which that world has changed since the 1960s.

1. The Supreme Court's decision in *New York Times v. Sullivan* in

1964 affirmed the proposition that under the First Amendment to the Constitution virtually nothing about a public figure is out of bounds to the press, provided it is not published with knowing or reckless disregard of its falsity. The Court's 1971 finding for the press in the Pentagon Papers case, while less definitive than *Times v. Sullivan,* was nevertheless perceived as a triumph for the press and the right to publish and a defeat for the theory of prior restraint on publishing, and thus punctuated *Times v. Sullivan* handsomely.[5]

Times v. Sullivan articulated First Amendment protection for criticism of public officials even when a news organization got some of the facts wrong, as was the case with a pro–civil rights advertisement in *The New York Times* that triggered the *Sullivan* suit. As Anthony Lewis has written, "the allowance of room for honest mistakes of fact encouraged the press, in particular, to challenge official truth on two subjects so hidden by government secrecy, Vietnam and Watergate, that no unauthorized story [about them] could ever have been" — as a traditional standard of libel required — "absolutely confirmable."[6]

2. And Vietnam and Watergate doubled as public crises, and disintegrations of presidential authority — personal collapses. In absorbing all this the press, deferential for so long toward the White House, acted as the people's surrogate. It began to operate according to the cautionary wisdom of old, "Fool me once, shame on you; fool me twice, shame on me." In particular, the tapes of Richard Nixon's private scheming with his advisers had a devastating effect on his public standing. As Michael Schudson has written, "The president's talk was foul, vengeful, full of ethnic slurs; it was particularly shocking to morally upright Republicans."[7]

3. The other element of language as dynamite in Watergate was the relentless news reporting of Bob Woodward and Carl Bernstein of *The Washington Post,* reflecting a dramatic, if transient, power shift from officialdom to the press. The fine movie based on Woodward and Bernstein's book, *All the Presidents' Men,* opens and closes with the sound and image of teletype pounding out the reporters' words, ultimately drowning out the cannon fire at Nixon's second inaugural. Those who controlled the words had achieved the power and, it seemed, the duty to probe and question to the core

those elected to manage the national destiny. Pen trumped sword — or so it appeared.

4. After Nixon's resignation came the pardon, by Ford, of Nixon. It was inevitable that the 1976 campaign would focus on a reaffirmation of morality and character. "I'll never lie to you," said Jimmy Carter.

This reaffirmation bred in the press not a new sense of balance in making judgments but rather a deepening of the presumption of suspicion and mistrust. Ben Bradlee of *The Washington Post* noted sardonically the spirit of the times in the newsroom: young reporters were covering "the most routine rural fires as if they were Watergate and would come back and argue that there was gasoline in the hose and the fire chief was an anti-Semite and they really thought that was the way to fame and glory." Bob Woodward explained his attitude about a peccadillo involving the Carter White House this way: "You have to remember that our experience for the past ten or fifteen years has been that in the end the government official always ended up being guilty as charged."[8]

5. The sexual revolution of the 1960s and 1970s lowered the barriers of admissibility of all sorts of personal behavior and categories of discussion in public print and over the air. It also brought women into the workforce in general and the newsroom in particular, breaking up the old men's club evoked in Alsop's account of the purposes of dinner with the powerful. (Indeed it was at her close friend Joe Alsop's home that Katharine Graham — as she recalled in her memoirs — forced the end of the Washington elite's rule that women retired "upstairs" at the end of the meal, while men of influence got serious over brandy and cigars.)[9]

6. In 1969 Edward Kennedy, who seemed poised for a blood-line inheritance of the presidency, disqualified himself for that trust for life at Chappaquiddick and then dissembled about what had happened. Under the new rules as well as the old, what was that about if not "character"?

7. Shocking posthumous revelations about the personal life of FDR . . . : In 1971, two years after Chappaquiddick, a year before Watergate, Joseph P. Lash published *Eleanor and Franklin,* bringing

the most godlike figure of the American Century closer to earth. The myth had held that it was FDR's polio that transformed his character and the Roosevelts' marriage. There had been previous allegations of his extramarital involvements, but now an authority friendly to the Roosevelts demonstrated that Eleanor's discovery in 1918 of Franklin's affair with her secretary, Lucy Mercer, had destroyed the marriage in all but facade and had been a crucial factor, along with the onset of FDR's polio in 1921, in the transformation of both Roosevelts — hitherto somewhat inconsequential individuals — into formidable but lonely public figures.

Lash's book forced a reestimation of Roosevelt the man, though for some it only underscored the extent to which a political leader should be measured on the basis of his public record rather than on that of his private life. For the revelation did not detract from FDR's accomplishments as president. Indeed, it and subsequent disclosures about his selfish and fickle behavior toward intimates argued for the theory that a truly great national leader must be capable of freeing him or herself from personal constraints and obligations. ("I was one of those who served his purposes," Eleanor Roosevelt had written with chilly stoicism after FDR's death.) Meanwhile, Lash's book helped raise questions about the veils contemporary powerful politicians wear in their lifetimes, and about the role of the press in conspiracies of silence, benign or otherwise.[10]

8. . . . and of JFK: Congressional investigations of the Nixon administration's uses of the CIA and FBI in the aftermath of Watergate uncovered, by the way, John F. Kennedy's embassies to and from the Mafia and his White House dalliances with a Mafia don's girlfriend. These tales were shocking in their details, but the sexual content was not new to the press corps or to political insiders in theme.

What the press had to contend with in the 1970s and 1980s was its own complicity in Kennedy's double life in the 1960s. Robert Pierpoint, then of CBS News: "There was quite a bit of discussion in the [Kennedy-era] White House press corps about how we should handle this. It was an ethical problem of concern to us in part because he was fairly blatant about it. But overall our basic feeling was that we shouldn't touch it because it wasn't our business or the public's business." David Broder of *The Washington Post*: "One of Kennedy's techniques for dealing with the press was to say things that were so damn candid — to some about sexual things but even his political comments — so that you knew if you printed it, you would be ending your intimate relationship.... It was a way of co-opting us."[11]

Journalists had, after all, been part of an elaborate wink in which the press assisted, if by indirection. Kennedy's "charisma," as the press had called it, came in several parts, and one of them was an aura of sexual excitement, a reputation for breaking all manner of taboos. Norman Mailer's celebration of Kennedy's cool, hip, suavely ruthless style in a memorable *Esquire* essay in 1960, "Superman Comes to the Supermarket" (and in a fictional treatment of such a politician, part JFK, part Mailer, in his 1965 novel *An American Dream*), had helped position Kennedy in contrast to the dull presidential style of the Eisenhower years. Such treatment also helped set the tone for a time — the "swinging sixties" — when a modulated buzz about a powerful politician's sex life became par for the course, a certification of "charisma." (That Nixon was an exception to this rule was evidence back then, for journalists and insiders, of a twisted inner life.)[12]

If Mailer's "literary" treatment of Kennedy as a hip, amoral, early postmodern hero set the tone for the 1960s, the young historian Michael Beschloss, in *The Crisis Years: Kennedy and Khrushchev, 1960–1963,* set the tone for the 1990s. Compounding the post-Watergate revelations about Kennedy's Mafia mistress, Beschloss wove the troubling, often astoundingly brazen record of Kennedy's private behavior as president into the fabric of diplomatic history so as to leap past the filtered treatments of the man by biographers and historians sympathetic to him, as well as by single-minded detractors. Beschloss showed how closely interwoven the two sides of Kennedy's life were; how obsessive and intrusive on the presidential schedule his sexual liaisons were; that as to liaisons in real time, Kennedy was vulnerable to blackmail by foreign governments, the Mafia, and J. Edgar Hoover of the FBI. Additionally, he showed, Kennedy's amphetamine-based treatments by a café society "Dr. Feelgood" may have affected his diplomacy.

Beschloss's presentation of the case of Kennedy was one in which the pieces of the life did *not* separate out, public and private. They had to be weighed together to reach a balanced evaluation of his presidency.[13]

9. Those were the more obvious reasons, occasions, and justifications for a new aggressiveness on the part of the press in probing public figures' private lives. Together with the movements in the streets, on campuses, and through American society and culture that broke down bias and opened up institutions in the 1960s, they added up to a profound contemporary distrust of establishments and a commitment to disclosure.

But the more systemic process discussed in the previous chapter was also at work: the paralysis of governance and collapse of the political parties.

The "opening" of politics after 1968 was diverting theater for a few election cycles: new faces, new rules, breathless suspense about the primary-of-the-week, stunning upsets, next round of press excitement. But behind the televised game show there was less and less that met the eye as to real government.

For simultaneous with the post-1968 political cleansings were the elements of malaise accumulating on top of the traumas of assassinations, Vietnam, and Watergate: economic erosion, deep inflation, immobilizing deficits, and governmental atrophy. Congress ceased to legislate daring new reforms, presidents (with the exception of Reagan and his tax cuts) to declare war on problems with much more than words. Cabinet members, once figures of note, became nonentities and time servers. The Senate and House, once the haunt of statesmen as well as politicians, were overrun by the merely well coiffed and telegenic.

If government doesn't work to meaningful effect, what its top elected officials and those aspiring to their positions do is ride economic waves up and down, and act out roles that are as transient as the next shift in economic indicators or the next round of pollsters' findings and prescriptions for their clients' "themes." If the parties don't matter, what politicians do is perform onstage and, offstage, attend personal fund-raisers to finance the new media-driven politics. The more the job description has to do with staged performance and the less it has to do with context, structure, substance, the more the press tends to treat officeholders and candidates as mere actors — "personalities." And the more it's inclined to rate their work according to estimations of how well they manage those personalities.

BACK WHEN GOVERNMENT was a churning engine of production, before its slide toward dysfunction and charade, the bond of trust that existed between press and the peers of officialdom was real. By the same token, a powerful and effective leader might be known all over town as a rogue, but if his effectiveness yielded notable results, those counted for more than his roguishness. Lyndon Johnson in the pre-Vietnam phases of his career is an example.

The Scotty Restons and Ed Murrows covered not only the heroic figures and menacing demagogues of their era; there were charlatans and clowns in abundance then, too. The difference is that today's political journalists operate in an environment in which there are few if any heroic figures to cover, few Marshall Plan or Great Society enterprises to report on, and that much more charlatanism, playacting, and time serving to expose. The respected and able technician — a James Baker, a Robert Rubin — absorbs residual attention as the exception proving the rule. Those who do the covering therefore look, and are sometimes susceptible to feeling, that much more towering themselves.

Of his role as what came to be called a "character cop" in the 1988 presidential campaign, Paul Taylor of *The Washington Post* wrote, "We are reporters in an age when personality and image dominate politics the way party and ideology once did. This shift has had everything to do with the ubiquity and intrusiveness of modern communications technology. It is beside the point to argue whether the change has been for the better. One can not uninvent television. . . . Nor can one wish away the simple truth that as our culture has become more media-soaked, the way we conduct political campaigns and measure political leaders has become more personality-soaked."

True enough. But therefore, Taylor continued, self-importance rising to the occasion, "somebody had to prune the field, to 'get rid of the funny ones,' as one 1988 campaign manager put it. It simply wasn't practical for voters to make choices among a dozen or more contenders."[14]

ON THE NIGHT of Saturday, May 2, 1987, four reporters and a photographer from *The Miami Herald*, acting on a tip that Gary Hart was due for an assignation with a young woman, staked out his home in Washington, D.C. On the basis of the stakeout (which all accounts now agree was incomplete), the *Herald* ran a story the next day across the top of its front page that began, "Gary Hart, the Democratic presidential candidate who has dismissed allegations of womanizing, spent Friday night and most of Saturday in his Capitol Hill town house with a young woman who flew from Miami and met him. Hart denied any impropriety." The same day, *The New York Times Magazine* ran a profile of Hart that quoted him saying of the media's interest in his private life, "Follow me around. I don't care. I'm serious. If anyone wants to put a tail on me, go ahead. They'd be very bored."[15]

The woman's name, Donna Rice, and the fact that she had earlier traveled to Bimini with Hart on a boat called the *Monkey Business*, quickly became the stuff of infamy. Former *Philadelphia Inquirer* reporter Richard Ben Cramer evoked the madness that ensued:

> That sent the [journalistic] pack over the edge. It was feral. It was without thought. Hart was catching the dread and fatal affliction—he was ridiculous. Even callow wannabe-big-feet could smell blood on the forest floor. Someone was gonna . . . *take Hart down*. . . . There was ineluctable logic to the chase: Hart was on the run. They had to show him embattled, fighting the iron ring, or dodging the cameras. That just meant more cameras, more bodies straining in the scrum, more fights, more noise, more video-rodeo to get the tape of Hart fleeing . . . which, of course, only made him more furtive, the hunted beast.

Meanwhile, *The Washington Post* had information, including a private detective's report, that Hart had been involved with yet another woman as recently as the previous December. Next stop, a press conference in Hanover, New Hampshire, three days after the

Herald story ran. Cramer's version: "The room should have held eighty to a hundred, but the pack was two-hundred strong . . . and, of course, there were tripods, cables, long lenses banging shoulders and skulls of the newsmen nearby, boom mikes poking crazily toward the front of the room, lights ablaze on spindly poles or burning hot white on the shoulders of the cameramen. It had to be a hundred degrees. . . . People in smelly suits, sweating, waiting . . . like a New York summer subway, stuck in the tunnel . . . *C'MON* . . . *Whatsa HOLDUP?*"

Post reporter Paul Taylor, he of the justification of eliminating "the funny ones" from the field, put to Hart the scarlet question, "Have you ever committed adultery?" Signals from Taylor and his editors (including Ben Bradlee) to Hart's high command then conveyed the message that if Hart withdrew from the race, the *Post* would not run its story about his other liaison. Hart left the race two days later.[16]

The resolution of the Hart case projected *The Miami Herald* and *The Washington Post,* and by extension the rest of the press, as virtual law enforcement officers unto themselves: First the *Herald's* stakeout (investigator). Second, Taylor's invidious question, "Have you ever committed adultery?" and subsequent justification — "What I did was ask Gary Hart the question he asked for" — (prosecutor). Third, the *Post's* role in Hart's abandonment of his candidacy (judge of the court imposing settlement).

There were objections. Suzanne Garment wrote in *The Wall Street Journal,* "Journalists had taken the front-runner for a major party's presidential nomination and made him history in a breathtakingly swift and direct way, without the need of intervention by voters or other politicians." Three *New York Times* columnists spanning the ideological spectrum, Anthony Lewis, A. M. Rosenthal, and William Safire, expressed disgust. Lewis: "When I read about *The Miami Herald* story on Gary Hart, I felt degraded in my profession." Rosenthal: "I did not become a newspaperman to hide outside a politician's house to find out whether he was in bed with somebody." Safire wrote that, had he been asked the adultery question, he would have replied, "Go to hell."[17]

They wrote as columnists, off the front lines of journalistic rough and tumble. But Taylor's own colleague on the reporting staff of the *Post*, the late Bill Peterson, refused to join him in working on the story of Hart's romantic involvements. Taylor himself recalled, "He thought the hour was late, the tip was weak and the story was sleazy. He worried that we were setting a precedent that could take us into the bedrooms of every other presidential candidate. I said this was a special case; the circumstances left us no choice; etc. But as I heard myself yammering, I realized — and it came as a shock — that there was more than one perspective on all this, even within my own shop."[18]

Within the profession, however, these doubts reflected minority views. The weight of opinion among working journalists was that stakeouts are a part of getting the news, that leads must be followed, and the news published.

There are lingering ironies from the Hart case: Hart's modeling of himself (like Bill Clinton) on John F. Kennedy, and his adoption (like Clinton) of the reckless corollary notion that he could, on the Kennedy plan, philander and get away with it; that some of *The Washington Post*'s insight into the candidate's persona derived from the fact that Hart had, during one of his separations from his wife, Lee, briefly rented an apartment in the house of Bob Woodward of Watergate fame; Ben Bradlee, intimate of JFK, nemesis of Nixon, and the force Hart had to answer to or yield to, personifies the post-Watergate institutional power of the press, and Hart the disintegration of political structure. (Hart was the product of no strong political organization or faction but rather of the amateurish McGovern campaign of 1972. Arguably the ablest and best-versed Democratic candidate for the 1988 nomination as to national and international issues, he was a phenomenon of the new politics, a telegenic loner.)

And finally, the late returns on the whole affair revealed gaps in the *Herald* reporters' stakeout — they hadn't covered all the doors to Hart's house all the time — and therefore in the authoritativeness of their story. In a careful reconstruction of the events for a book about the 1988 campaign, two respected reporters, Jack Germond of *The*

Baltimore Sun and Jules Witcover of *The Washington Post,* left room for the possibility that Rice's denials that she had spent the fateful night at Hart's house, or had gone to bed with him, were credible. Hanged for a sheep or a goat?[19]

The Hart case is notable for its excesses of behavior on the parts of both politician and press, and for what followed in the form of press ambivalence about its own uncertain role in the new trip-wire political environment. Paul Taylor of the *Post* himself recorded one more irony, though it may be read differently than he hoped. Back at *The Washington Post* editor Bradlee quizzed reporter Taylor about the events in New Hampshire:

" 'You were the one who asked that question?'
" 'Yeah,' I said, half expecting a high-five.
"Bradlee rolled his eyes and said 'Shee-yit!'
"As eye rolls go, this one was ambiguous — conveying surprise more than approval or disapproval. Or so I'd like to think. I've made it a point never to ask."[20]

OFF THE CAMPAIGN trail, there followed quick ends to the public careers of two other powerful figures, their private lives laid out in the press with help from partisan, malicious sources. These were Democratic Speaker of the House of Representatives Jim Wright and Republican secretary of defense–designate John Tower. Revenge was in the air; the overall climate invited metaphors of the hunt, the kill, and the meal. "I'm very concerned about what's happening to government," Republican senator John Danforth of Missouri had said about an earlier episode, involving Jimmy Carter's budget director, Bert Lance. "I think we're eating ourselves alive."[21]

The atmosphere was the more poisonous because, after the Hart scandal, news organizations were less certain than ever about how to deal with tips, leaks, and salacious stories. Political operatives knew this. Shortly after the political demise of Wright and Tower, *The New York Times* reported that many journalists "are concerned about the degree to which they are manipulated by politicians on the attack, and they worry that the pressure resulting from competition among news organizations can lead to a lowering of standards of inquiry."[22]

"We are moving these days into areas of great uncertainty," wrote Anna Quindlen in *The New York Times,* deploring the journalistic climate that led in 1992 to the disclosure of Arthur Ashe's AIDS condition against his wishes. "We are making a lot of this up as we go along."[23]

Compounding journalism's dilemma about the application of professional standards was the raising of the stakes. That is, vastly increased vulnerability for public figures carries with it vastly enhanced firepower for journalists.

"They can't touch me while I'm alive," Kennedy was reported to have said of his scandalous behavior, "and after I'm dead, who cares?" That was then. Now, a careful historian like Beschloss attempts to answer the question of character after a passage of time and assessment of archives as well as sources' testimony. Today's journalist faces another dilemma entirely in trying to report on character as revealed in the present, with dramatic effect on lives and events in the here and now.[24]

The press did not invent the character issue in American politics. It traces back to the blood feuds among Hamilton, Jefferson, and Aaron Burr, by way of those among Andrew Jackson, John Quincy Adams, and Henry Clay. But in its contemporary, indiscriminate, and obsessive forms, it's a function of the disintegration of American politics. And as historian Alan Brinkley wrote at the time of the Hart scandal, until a political leader finds an effective counter to "the sense of aimlessness and emptiness that afflicts American public life . . . we are likely to continue to judge our leaders by scrutinizing and at times repudiating them on the basis of the one thing they offer us: themselves."[25]

Brinkley's words anticipated the press and the public's convoluted relationship with Bill Clinton a full four years before Clinton loomed as a national figure.

IN THE 1984 Democratic presidential primaries the stolid warhorse candidate, Walter Mondale, upstaged the more sprightly Gary Hart, candidate of vaguely articulated "new ideas," with the down-to-earth challenge "Where's the beef?" In fact Hart was one of the more serious figures in the Senate, hard working, well staffed, expert on national security issues. Hart and his handlers puffed up such incisiveness into a "new ideas" campaign posture that was indeed heavy on imagery, but it was Mondale who relied on an advertising wisecrack to deflate him.

By contrast Bill Clinton, out of Arkansas by way of television, was a self-manufactured candidate whose imagery included a well-displayed passion for the appearance of command of policy issues, real depth in no area at all, unruly appetites, tendencies to narcissism and dissembling, and a raging fixation on the Kennedy aura that made Gary Hart's identification with JFK seem merely platonic.[26]

In the political culture of the times, which is to say the media culture of the times, Clinton's quirks swiftly became identifying marks for a public increasingly attuned, thanks to television and pop psychology, to dysfunction on parade. Where national politicians like Fritz Mondale, Michael Dukakis, and George Bush had reinforced the public's boredom with politics, Clinton offered a bizarre family history, pathology and misbehavior visible to all, combined with disarming acting skill and matchless talk-show know-how—a crowd-pleasing combination for a public addicted to tabloid television fare.

But many in the press smelled trouble. As the investigation into the Clintons' Whitewater dealings accelerated at the start of the president's second year in office, R. W. Apple wrote in *The New York Times,* "Like Mr. Nixon, Mr. Clinton is vulnerable in a crisis of this sort because of the ambiguous reputation that preceded him into Presidential politics. . . . One brought the nickname 'Tricky Dick' into the Oval Office, the other 'Slick Willy.' "[27]

The press was tacking, as it usually does, on a course of self-correction. Sensitive to the backlash against its active role in the liquidation of Gary Hart in 1987, the press had been inclined to downgrade the importance of candidate Clinton's involvement with Gennifer Flowers when the story surfaced early in 1992. Thereafter, as Clinton's Pinocchio problem and inconstancy revealed themselves as second nature in his handling of his draft history and other matters, opinion leaders in the press tacked back to a view that they'd given Clinton too great a benefit of the doubt.

AN ARTICULATED DEFENSE of Clinton came in his first two years on the national scene in two forms. Both were heavily condemnatory of the press.

One, advanced by commentators like communications scholar Jay Rosen of New York University, rehearsed the theme of the press as watchdog gone rabid, overprimed on its own "savviness," which Rosen called "amoral . . . , a propaganda of the uncommitted" that makes politics "a game of power fought by clever insiders and master strategists, a running scorecard of winners and (mostly) losers, a theater of contempt, a nightly joke." Gamely, Rosen defended Clinton's "politics of hope" and Hillary Rodham Clinton's "politics of meaning" as antidotes to contemporary cynicism.[28]

A second defense came from liberal journalists and policy experts who saw Clinton, however flawed, as having the outside-man skill to retake command of American politics from the heirs to Ronald Reagan. In addition, Clinton had an insider orientation to what one of those supporters, Sidney Blumenthal, called "the Conversation." This, wrote Blumenthal in *The New Republic,* was a dialogue among members of "a new Democratic establishment that has never really wielded national power but impatiently wants its chance in the aftermath of Reaganism," a generationally eager project to "rethink . . . the future of liberalism and the Democratic Party that [Clinton] and his wife have been part of for years."

"Clinton seeks accurate, immediate, politically sensitive transmission of his policies," wrote Blumenthal in *The New Yorker* in 1993. "The national press, and especially the network news, is too blunt, too unfocused, too superficial. It is inadequate at both ends of the political spectrum: not only is it unable to provide intense immediacy to specific groups and places but its compulsive reduction of reality to soundbite dimensions makes it incapable of carrying broad, sustained explanation."

With approval, Blumenthal cited Clinton in gleeful defiance of a black-tie dinner audience of broadcast journalists that year: "You know why I can stiff you . . . [in not scheduling televised] press conferences? . . . Because Larry King liberated me by giving me to the American people directly."

The forces of the New Right, with their smart media techniques and use of fax and Internet, are much more influential and effective than you of the press and political elites have the wit to know (went the subtext of Blumenthal's argument). Beating them requires a candidate who can outmaneuver them at the media game. So move over, hold your tongues, and let the next generation have its turn, make its mistakes, learn from them. (With no shortage of enemies in the Washington press corps, Blumenthal took the ultimate step of putting his professional capital where his mouth was by joining the Clinton administration as senior adviser to the president in 1997.)[29]

Despite their plausibility, these rationales for Clinton were thin in the eyes of his critics in the press and among sophisticated elites. For Clinton's first and final commitment was to his own maneuverability, which meant his ability to dissemble, abandon allies, intimates, and positions taken, and pop up smiling some yards distanced from the trouble lately besetting him. Franklin Roosevelt did the same, but FDR had a vibrant coalition party politics and thriving engines of government working for him, buttressing him, helping to depersonalize his maneuvers and tacks. As time passed, the press looked at Clinton and saw not the Rosen or Blumenthal arguments or the remotest shadow of Franklin Roosevelt, but the scheming Dick Morris, refashioning amorality for the New Age.

SO WHEN IN early 1998 the Monica Lewinsky scandal broke out of the investigation of the Clintons' Arkansas investments and alleged misdeeds in the White House, a logical press reaction was that the president had — as seemed fated — finally destroyed himself. The trail of presidential misbehavior this time was too blatant, the allegations too disgusting, the pathology too uncontrollable, the self-exculpatory charm and rationales too thin, to permit him escape.

A modern scandal (so went the press assumption) exists to be investigated. It's what the public demands (however much it protests otherwise) and what we of the press must do (which means allowing for some excess and short-cutting) lest the competition get there first and render us irrelevant.

To many reporters on the job adding factual detail to the story, press excess and susceptibility to managed leaks on all sides were secondary to the context: the easy virtue of the Clinton White House overall. Other investigations that season revealed disturbing Clinton campaign fund-raising abuses, including evidence that representatives of foreign interests were trading contributions for White House access and even decisions related to national security. The scorched-earth style of the White House response to its critics — an application of the Blumenthal doctrine that the right wing will get you if you don't get it first — fed press instincts that such a bloodthirsty defense only signaled the depth of the scandal.[30]

But a vast majority of the audience stayed on its own wavelength. It was shocked but also, after months of the scandal's domination of news and conversation, sated, and it was focused in any event on what had been, for once, good news: the booming economy. This was a new low for Clinton — what else was new? Certainly not that campaign corruption reached deep into the White House. As to scandal, *national* scandal engulfing everything, Watergate had marked a generation with the sense that the depths of communal disgust required by impeachment and removal from office are more searing than the scandal itself. As the more discerning interpretations of Clinton's poll ratings in the face of the scandal took care to note, the public was not exactly in "support" of the president. Instead, it wished that the Clinton sex scandal would cease to upstage the usual mundane news about campaign finance chicanery and the like, forcing the language of crisis into headlines, triggering anxiety about national stability and boom times.[31]

HERE WAS A cultural stalemate. The press, like the independent prosecutor, was ablaze with devastating evidence of the truth about Clinton's character. The majority of the audience already knew about Bill Clinton's character. It knew that misbehavior was his middle name. It was not prepared to deal with the proposition that what constituted Clinton's character flaws — his seductive, chameleonlike personality, his adolescent appetites, his stated mantra ("deny, deny, deny") — were precisely what made him so successful in the modern presidency's "permanent campaign." What mattered was his cool mastery of the newly conglomerated political, media, and entertainment cultures. What mattered was his appearance of being able to ride out storms — and his secretary of the treasury's appearance of being able to keep foreign economic distress from the nation's markets. In other circumstances, Clinton might be seen to be part of the problem. For the moment, he seemed to be part of what was keeping the problem at bay. So investigative zeal and critical judgment met the inertia of a public nervous about disruption.

In the wake of the Clinton-Lewinsky scandal, the press appeared to know less than the public what to do with the character issue. It had seemed to learn from the Gary Hart case that trying to cover "character" when you mean "sex life" can make for a dangerously double-edged sword. But what besides character was there to track in the new political environment? What's a watchdog to do?

For all its soul-searching, its ambivalence about its own performance, the press — "making a lot of this up as we go along" — groped along with the other principal players for a purchase on the barren and slippery new political slope.

SIX

Private Lives

THE SOAP-OPERATIC CYCLES of preoccupation with public officials' character, featuring the press in the role of ever skeptical "character cop," was a reflection of the drift of American political life from coherence to trivialized instability. The erosion of effective governance and of rooted political parties were the structural factors in that drift, overlooked amid the finger-pointing at (and within) the press. But what about the audience's reaction to the drama — and participation in it? How could there be a drama, let alone a mass market melodrama, without an audience?

The audience, considered en masse or in its subcategories, was hard to know. Those who focused on the sorry state of the parties and of public disaffection with them tended to be good, gray, and far from the streets. They were high-minded alumni of reform campaigns, sober, reflective newspaper journalists like David Broder and E. J. Dionne. Their reports, op-ed page columns, and books deplored the decline of citizens' connection to "public life" and the ascendancy of shrill ideologies. They prescribed remedies for the growing distance between insiders in the political game and the public. But the thrust of their work focused on the political arena; it did not explore the shifts in American society, condition, and zeitgeist.[1]

That left detective work about the audience to the functionaries of the opinion polling industry.

THE FADING OF dynamic governance and decline of an engaged party politics from their traditional place in American life lacked a coherent story line. Like fog, the vagaries of the new "image politics" crept in on a culture used to story lines on the order of defeating the Axis powers, saving the peace, waging the Cold War, ending racial segregation, wiping out poverty, exploring outer space, and, in the late 1960s and early 1970s, ending the Vietnam War and reforming "the system."

In place of such narrative coherence, pollsters and media consultants in recent decades have floated kaleidoscopic schematics highlighting "values" both sanctified ("trust," "family") and demonized ("liberalism") and emotions (principally fear and anger) of concern to targetable social groupings ("soccer moms," Baby Boomers). The news business followed suit, trying at least to follow the indicators of growing anxiety about economic security. But apart from these labels and threads, and despite the cult of survey research and focus groups, audiences for news were essentially faceless to most journalists.

They were faceless in that most of those surveys asked people questions and processed responses in the absence of informed historical, sociological, or psychological assessment of who they were, of the nature of their odysseys, of their and the nation's history. The survey questions and answers were, in trade lingo, "snapshots in time" for the purpose of assessing "mood" and "theme." Their principal application was by politicians campaigning, officials maintaining their ratings, and journalists tracking the success rate of such marketing activity.

Did use of them assist the press in informing the public? Sometimes yes, sometimes no. The most basic psychological training would have taught that the more painful or subtle or sensitive the question on the table—about the United States' reversals in the 1960s and 1970s, about the roots of public anxiety and alienation, about sexual behavior—the more tentative, self-protective, and faceless the response would be.

"People who seemed ready to scale the political ramparts a few years ago are looking more like democracy's couch potatoes, just watching passively," intoned a *Wall Street Journal* front-page report, drawing on its polling conducted in tandem with NBC News but ducking the question "whether this detachment is a simply a passing phase or a sign of permanent changes." ("Odds are, it's a bit of both.") The more polling as deus ex machina invaded the practice of politics and journalism in a time of confusion and loss, the more it, too, helped fill out the space that leadership on one hand and active, grass-roots participation in political party life on the other had previously taken. And the less it was probed for nuance or taken with salt.[2]

Furthermore, the practice of surveying in a historical vacuum deepened the difficulty the press had in making sophisticated connections between what was happening to our politics and the turning of audiences away from news. Typically, a *New York Times* report based on a poll conducted jointly with CBS News on the eve of the 1994 congressional elections could both report widespread public disgust with politics and state that "the poll showed no relationship between voters' sources of news and their level of cynicism, pessimism or alienation from the political process." Such reliance on polling in and of itself helped perpetuate syndromes of both skin-deep news coverage about the public mood and loss of public engagement with the news.[3]

THROUGH THE ASSASSINATIONS, riots, reverses, outright defeats, and disintegration of the 1960s and early 1970s, millions and millions of Americans had been cumulatively robbed of hopes, dreams, promises, structures. The gains then and later — the rights revolution (as it's been called), the end of the Cold War, an economic boom — were real enough considered in isolation. But for many, the full enjoyment of enhanced rights and boom times was blunted by such elements of loss as inflation, urban decay, the rustbelt effect, and onset of systemic economic insecurities.

Most seriously for the press, the severing of the link for so many people between "the news" and the idea that it was relevant had already happened. All too many forces that accompanied the years of greatest loss — the cultural shifts, the decomposition of politics, the emergence of new technologies connected to "do your own thing" forms of recreation — stood in the way of restoration of that link. So private life played out, in contrast to the ways it had in previous decades, in an atmosphere of ever greater loss of connection to public life.

Thoughtful journalists were quick enough to understand at least that they were prominent among the agents of loss. But that perception tended to be situational: individual journalists understood it as a professional dilemma and, if there were enough minutes or hours in the day, as a reflection of the times. Several news organizations, notably *The Philadelphia Inquirer* in its sequence of reports on governance and the middle class beginning in 1991, mounted probes into the modern condition. But these were initiatives far out of the ordinary.

For the news business as an institution to have gone deep into the roots of contemporary public anxiety, pain, and outright anger would have risked recognition of a specter the industry was not ready to confront. That is, rampant public alienation was taking many forms, one of which was the loss of a broad, committed, mass audience for journalism. To have explored the phenomenon in depth would have brought the news business face to face with its fundamental dilemma; with a cloaked but dominant story of our time and the riddle of how to deal with it. Failure to do so perpetuated the blindness of the press in trying to lead the blind. Much safer in news business conclaves, much less taxing all around, to talk of lifestyle choices putting a claim on "people's time."[4]

IN FACT, IT'S the youngest, greenest cub reporter who often comes face to face with the conflicted nuances of audience attitudes. For such younger journalists generally inherit the sticky task of asking the stricken parent, child, wife, husband, or friend for details and pictures of the loved one who has been kidnapped, killed, indicted, or otherwise caught in the headlights of onrushing news.

To the extent that the person interviewed can accept the news story as one of the inevitable effects of the event, she or he will want the reported details to be faithful to the facts, at least to the extent of not compounding pain with inaccuracy or distortion. And people in such circumstances sometimes find the sharing of the details, the processing of the loss, cathartic and comforting.

On the other hand, the person interviewed resents the fact of the story, as a function of the disaster for which it stands. And no doubt there is inevitably some fault to be found with the tone the story will strike, the judgments it will imply, the boundaries it will cross, or the detail it will bungle no matter how hard the reporter tries to get everything right.

On the other side of the line, that green reporter, feeling empathy and working to win the interviewee's confidence, must learn detachment and skepticism, especially when a story touches close to home. If she or he is a slow learner, a grizzled editor will drill it in. "If your mother says she loves you," goes the old maxim of Chicago journalism, "check it out."

Good journalists assimilate these basic training lessons in ways that help them make balanced decisions about such tensions later in their careers. And depending on how well they make those decisions, they affect overnight the lives of others with more, or less, unpleasant aftertaste. That aftertaste turns up in the opinion surveys, not always articulately stated, as part of the count against the press on the arrogance charge. It's an attitude that can spring from the most inconsequential personal connection to a news story, as well as from entrapment in or near a full-blown, melodramatic collision between private life and news.

What a reader or viewer feels for a Bill Clinton or a Clarence Thomas or an Anita Hill, a Gary Hart or an Arthur Ashe, or those close to them becomes a blur of fascination, doubt about the legitimacy of the fascination, questions about the power of the searchlight. And what a journalist attempting to report or edit such a story feels while attempting to manage the spotlight becomes its own blur of conflicting values.

I'VE SPENT MY share of difficult hours with colleagues in and out of the newsroom deciding whether to reveal a famous politician's indiscretion, whether to identify a prominent citizen's death as a suicide, whether to name relatives caught up in a public figure's imbroglio — and wondering how our news would sit with our audience.

At *The Boston Globe* early in 1984 we had advance word of Massachusetts Democratic senator Paul Tsongas's decision to leave office for reasons of health, which turned out to be a diagnosis of lymphoma. But the senator wanted to break the news on his own timetable (which included talking through his hopeful near-term prognosis with his young daughters before they experienced the shock of the words "cancer" and "Tsongas" linked in black headlines and television images). What to do?

As usually happens at such a moment, reporters and editors argued whether to go with a disturbing story — this one about a well-liked public figure, one with whom the *Globe* had friendly relations. Meanwhile a member of the staff opened back-channel negotiations with the senator's politically astute twin sister, Thalia Slesinger, who pressed the argument that her brother's condition would inevitably be depicted as more dire than it was unless he was permitted to announce it on his terms — in other words, to maintain control of the story of his life.

The hawkish position in such a case is that it's the business of a news organization to publish the news, like it or not — period. In addition we had the semblance of a moral argument with which to counter the Tsongases' concerns: if we had the story the salaciously tabloid *Boston Herald* could not be far behind; we could guarantee that we would treat the story with sensitivity and safely predict the *Herald* would not. The argument from lesser evil seemed persuasive to me. In the end we worked out an arrangement whereby Tsongas announced the basic decision and diagnosis and gave the *Globe* an embargoed interview about the details of his diagnosis — which meant he had several days to talk those through with his daughters. And so the newsroom drama ended.[5]

I helped decide how to deal with several other stories, generally on the side of newsworthiness. But as with word of Tsongas's illness, I can call up as an instant reflex the mental and physical unease I felt then and sensed in others as we debated the nuances of the story a decade and a half ago.

THE MORAL AMBIGUITIES inherent in digging for news in a disintegrating political environment, with only the vaguest of boundaries between public and private spheres, extended far beyond the confines of in-house seminars in ethics. For the confusion, the flaw, the fault, lay not just with the press, nor with a trivialized political system. The problem was also society's; ours as human beings. Indeed, the confusion in the press about the boundaries of privacy was in great part a reflection of human ambivalence about privacy and secrets. This was the more so as the elements of the political environment that had worked as buffers — the parties — faded into the mist.

What "people" felt — that theoretically palpable "public opinion" that polls presumed to measure, and everyone to generalize about — in cases like Gary Hart's and Bill Clinton's was not much different from what they felt about events much closer to home. That is, the chaotic rush of emotions it is human nature to experience when mishap, misstep, or scandal occurs in the neighborhood or one's professional circle.

Who has not observed what plays out in such a setting, and measured it, if only in a flash, against what goes on in one's own head? That is, a mixture of fascination, regret, shock, shared discomfort, empathy, pity, good fortune not to be so afflicted, amusement, titillation, eagerness to hear all the details, passing shame about such smallness in oneself, wish that the whole affair would disappear and the clock be set back to before it began, anger at those who are gossiping salaciously; all of this at once and making no coherent sense. If feelings for the person on the spot are negative, a pinch of pleasure at comeuppance is of course added to the mix. But most of the other chemical properties are there, too; particularly shame at getting such a kick out of the degradation of scandal or the misfortune of others, at taking part in the casting of stones.

Thus the connections between a public figure's embarrassment and one's private reaction to it are many and interwoven. In the cases of Nixon, Hart, and Clinton as of the arrogant or reckless or hapless local high school principal or town clerk or office colleague enveloped in an ugly scandal, the unease of the person in trouble has the potential to become the unease of the community.

An individual in an interaction with others operates at some level of understanding of the "definition," or terms, of the interaction, the sociologist Erving Goffman has suggested. When unforeseen events throw that definition of the setting off, the individual "may feel ashamed while the others present may feel hostile," he wrote, "and all the participants may come to feel ill at ease, nonplussed, out of countenance, embarrassed, experiencing the kind of anomy that is generated when the minute social system of face-to-face interaction breaks down."[6]

In larger public situations, too, such communal embarrassment and the impulse to deal with it take on a life of their own. So the candidate or public official under fire calls a press conference to clear the air, to make amends or claim there's nothing to hide, to appeal that together we "get this issue behind us," and "move on." Reporters compete to pin the target of the scrutiny down in some new discrepancy. As the politician's embarrassment deepens, so do the complexities of the public's involvement with that embarrassment.

Nixon, author of a book on his own "crises," inept at managing face-to-face contact with the country in his Watergate embarrassment, had to go. So did Hart. Clinton, beneficiary of resentment against press excess in dispatching Hart, hung on, gravely wounded, brazenly evading the truth about allegations fated to emerge as factual, earning residual credit for unfazed management of his embarrassment and his exploitation of the conflicted swirl of public opinion about it.

Much of the public turned on the players fanning the flames. Joseph Lelyveld, executive editor of *The New York Times,* observed in the spring of 1998, "The spectacle, most people felt, embarrassed us as a country so, of course, when asked they said they wanted it to end. All those who kept it going — prosecutors, investigators, reporters, commentators — obviously were working against that desire." As the ordeal wore on, the public registered greater disgust with Clinton's antagonists' magnification of the scandal and with "the media" than with the scandal itself. This was a river of discontent within American politics in search of an outlet. One villain vindicated another; only a few seasons earlier the sorry choice for millions of voters had been between Clinton's cynicism about maintaining basic commitments and Bob Dole's failure to present himself as a convincing alternative.[7]

In lieu of a strong party and deep allegiance to it to support him in time of trouble, Clinton made the best of these amorphous circumstances. For all his shameless embarrassment, he had helped himself to a transient semblance of a new "party" alignment in the crisis. There was no Democratic position, save for the fact that Democrats in Congress were overwhelmingly disgusted with Clinton's behavior, lies about it, and net infliction of damage to their own fortunes. Many Republicans lay low. Filling the vacant adversary space was a Party of Righteousness. That made Clinton — all too human sinner — de facto leader of a Party of Good Times, the party of those who do not wish to be governed by righteous puritans, and those lately enjoying some prosperity. The legal and congressional processes might roll on, and the press similarly in coverage of them, but as long as the majority of the audience saw the "party" lines so moralistically drawn, Clinton — incredible, disgraced, impeached, alone — was safe.

IN PAST TIMES, the journalist covering the politician might see the latter as another breed. But as is still true of sportswriters covering athletes, journalists and politicians used to become friends by another name, or at least intimate acquaintances; people with whom one interacted intensely first-hand. The journalist might marvel at the politician's capacity for sheer solipsism or hypocrisy, sneer at the transparency of his sincerity, but he more than others knew his subject was "doing a job."

Contemplating the vacuity of the interactions, the journalist might conclude, as Russell Baker did, that he no longer wanted to spend his career "idling outside closed doors [in the corridors of the U.S. Senate] . . . waiting for somebody to come out and lie to me." But it was only the rare and unusually evil politician in disaster, self-inflicted or not, for whom the reflective journalist did not feel some residual mixed emotion. ("The poor son-of-a-bitch," the late Murray Kempton concluded a characteristically idiosyncratic reflection on Roy Cohn, of all people.)[8]

The contemporary public mind for its part was more often conflicted and nuanced than singular. The decline of meaningful party politics as a mediator of that nuance magnified journalism's problems as a stand-in. Accordingly, grand efforts to capture the dark side of the zeitgeist tended to wind up reductive and superficial;

thus, *Time* covered the 1992 election campaign with headlines fairly screaming "THE ANGRY VOTER" and "Voters Are Mad as Hell."[9]

Journalism's awkwardness with nuance invited a comparison of it to other forms. In his classic *Seven Types of Ambiguity,* the poet William Empson wrote of the seventh and most complex form of poetic ambiguity that it occurs when a word (like "character," for the sake of argument) has two meanings, and the author reveals the conflict between these two meanings, and in his own mind. For example, "the notion of what you want involves the idea that you have not got it . . . it marks a center of conflict; the notion of what you want involves the notion that you must not take it." And that is a way that journalists, in text and subtext, sought ever more frenetically to nail a public figure's "character," even as it eluded them.[10]

Sociologists, psychologists, poets, and philosophers are more comfortable reflecting on such aspects of the communications process than are journalists. Sissela Bok, who has written on lying and secrets, has mused on whether journalists and other professionals view secrets as "guilty" and "threatening," connoting impropriety, or "awesome and worthy of respect." She wrote that "it is almost as if the effort to define *secrecy* reflected the conflicting desires that approaching many an actual *secret* arouses: the cautious concern to leave it carefully sealed, or on the contrary, the determination to open it up, cut it down to size, see only one of its aspects, hasten to solve its riddle."[11]

The public partook of those conflicting desires, too.

THAT DUALITY IN the meaning of secrecy parallels a persistent tension in First Amendment law between freedom of expression (that is, the right to probe and speak) and the right to privacy. As the California Supreme Court once phrased it, "the right to know and the right to have others not know are, simplistically considered, irreconcilable." Complicating journalists' problems in grappling with the duality of secrets and the vagueness of privacy law were two more factors.[12]

One was the proliferation of channels of communication beyond the boundaries of organized journalism, from "trash TV" to the

Internet. The second was the absence of a coherent professional code or logical, let alone ethical, context for deciding questions of "character" and privacy. Together they promised a next wave of journalistic disaster: hoaxes or half-truths disseminated among audiences, perhaps on the Internet, perhaps involving doctored tape or film, unmediated by journalists in the first instance but compelling enough to demand further dissemination by them, with seriously harmful results to affected individuals.

With variations on the Nixon, Hart, Tower, Thomas, and Clinton themes, the stories of public figures' private embarrassment and squalor had come to assume a ritual quality, tracing back to the myths of antiquity. Here was an ambivalent Greek chorus representing the broad public, its mood shifting as revelations piled in. There was the press as shaman (as communications scholar Barbie Zelizer has suggested), empowered to go where others cannot and return with stories that have the effect of triggering communal embarrassment. Then, dramatic process takes over: front-page headlines signal the public figure's increasingly "untenable" position, raising the ante in pace with editorial-page calls for an end to the endgame. Gradually the press role as shaman shifts to that of exorcist. The press assumes the task of helping to force the communal embarrassment to a denouement, easing the audience's love-hate relationship with the scandal.[13]

This is a way to view the larger dynamic of which the press is only one part, otherwise reductively labeled a "feeding frenzy." Seen that way, those contradictory poll findings on public condemnation of an intrusive press back-to-back with residual support for a watchdog press make perfect sense.

When in the face of scandal the contemporary politician failed in the management of image and credible on-screen self-presentation, the audience needed an exorcist — and was unhappy it had that need. The public depended on the press to perform the work of ritual cleansing — and feared and resented the press for its power to do so. In other societies, these conflicts are manifest in such phenomena as show trials of the formerly high and mighty.

But lacking a broad awareness of the elements of the drama, the press was like an adolescent who has prematurely achieved height and strength. And so when the press as exorcist managed its role poorly and the hunted animal of a politician managed his effectively, the combustible substances were all in place, owing to audience prerogative, to consume the powerful exorcist rather than its sorry target.

ONE FURTHER WRINKLE to the pattern of journalistic power without self-knowledge, and that of the audience's ambivalence. As Bok argues, there is an absurd presumption in the cliché *the public's right to know*. A more precise, less pretentious phrasing would make it *the public's right of access to information*. A frequent corollary cliché was that public officials forfeit much, even all, of their right to privacy when they ask for our mandate to determine our fate. But rarely contemplated was the question of presumption to know how to measure that public figure's private self, to decide that "character issue."[14]

Indeed to this day the least known and truly measured inner characters in American history belong to two of our greatest and best loved presidents, Abraham Lincoln and Franklin Roosevelt. Linked to the American people beyond politics, at mystic levels, they remain mysteriously impenetrable and sibylline for all the words written about them. Arguably their mystique flowed in part from the fact that they exercised great power in times of crisis with extraordinary self-reliance, independent to a great extent of mentors or intimate advisers; there were simply not many witnesses to the nature of their inner selves. Moreover, a source of that self-reliance was their intuitive connection to a people in crisis, to "national will" at historical crossroads. They connected to the public in a manner at once transcendent and democratic.[15]

Neither kept diaries or lived to write memoirs. The deaths of each on the job, on the eve of resolution of epic undertakings, came as shocking losses to the public; in death they towered over the lesser men who succeeded them. Bok writes of the "unique [and] unfathomable" aspects of a human being, adding, "the death of an individual has been likened to the burning down of a great library or to a universe going extinct, as the inwardness and focus and connections of a life are lost, along with what William Blake called 'the holiness of minute particulars.' "[16]

Consider those images — burning library, dying universe — in the cases of Lincoln and Roosevelt. Then consider the fallacies inherent in the notion of the press trying to grapple with the ultimate "character" of such individuals.

PART 3

The Business

SEVEN

Bottom Line

FOR MORE THAN a century and a half, since the news business began to intersect with emerging technologies like the telegraph, railroads, and rapid-speed printing, it has chronicled — and reflected in its own growth — the evolution of American society from rural and small-town existence to urban, and then suburban, social organization. Similarly, the development of the American press was integral with the nation's assimilation of waves of immigration and its transit from preoccupation with American separateness to entry onto the international stage as a great power. On up to the present, few if any industries could identify themselves more thoroughly or more credibly than the news business both as representatives of the society in which they operated and as principal interpreters of news and information back to that society.

Then, suddenly, in the last third of the twentieth century, as American fortunes waned, technology made possible news, on television, in real time. The acceleration of the news cycle cut into the ability of the news business to reflect on what it was doing, to edit and to think. The ascendancy of television usurped the old journalistic order, and the political one as well, pushing aside the arrangement of words in sentences in stories displayed in relation to one another in favor of visual effect and the craft of image management. Just how much was a local or metropolitan newspaper (or a national newsmagazine) worth in a media environment defined for many by worldwide cable news "all the time"?

Gone was the orderly, set-piece press conference or speech,

replaced by the mobile camera and mike, by fast-cutting and weaving of film. What had been several-days-old film from the front in television news during the Vietnam years became live-action film in the 1980s and 1990s (except when the Pentagon closed it down, as in the Persian Gulf War).

In 1993 a conference of past and present government officials and journalists discussing the impact of television news on foreign policy making concluded that thanks to "the CNN effect" — a ubiquitous TV news presence at points of crisis — the Cuban missile crisis of 1962 could not possibly be managed offstage today as it was then. The trigger effects of televised film of the Rodney King beating and the verdict in the case of the policemen who beat him demonstrated the extent to which "the media" could themselves become an anarchic force in the news, as distinct from the interpreters of it.[1]

Journalism's expanded impact both attracted and disturbed people. The press was more instantaneous, yes; it could dig deeper, faster, leap more nimbly around the world, revealing more, yes; but it could also tell us more than we want, on reflection, to know; cause more damage, set off more secondary effects. These were all causes for mounting expressions of fear and resentment of the dark carnival of "media," undifferentiated from the responsible press. So was the proliferation of television "newsmagazines" and talk shows that trafficked in news for the purpose of entertaining, many of them with the slimmest of connections to the standards saluted by professional journalists.

These trends drew ritual condemnations of pandering to tabloid taste and the ratings game. More elusive was the proposition that as to public interest, beyond post-Vietnam and post-Watergate fatigue and escapism lay a what-the-hell postmodernism, if a more literal version than that practiced by artists and satirists. According to it, neither history nor the future — news — mattered much, and the present was to be endured. The "media" bazaar in its ever more tabloid and entertainment orientations made endurance that much more endurable.

And so, after more than 150 years in which its own expansionary progress had been dynamically interwoven with that of the United States itself, those paid to think about the future of the news business were struggling awkwardly with such primal realities as time, distance, privacy, relevance, and the fundamentals of contemporary culture.

IT BECOMES CLEARER that, for the press as for average citizens, in the years since the 1960s the story of our time has shifted in its narrative drive from being (with the important qualifications before the 1960s and since then noted earlier) a "good news" story to being a "bad news" story.

As noted, that is not to gloss over the searing events or political depravity — McCarthyism, the Cold War, the nuclear nightmare — of earlier decades. Rather, it's to argue that the overarching narrative about America from the end of the Depression well into the 1960s, the story the press told, was on the whole of a people and a government equal to challenges. More than equal, for success bred a shared national confidence, pride, motivation to meet the next challenge.

An exclusive, racist society? It was in the "complacent" 1950s as well as in the "activist" 1960s that the leaders of American political institutions, along with the American people, pressured effectively by those on the outside wanting in, faced the charge of racial inequality and began to come to consensus about the need to right wrongs.[2]

Offer the good news of recent years (call it transient or long-term): lowered barriers for women and racial minorities seeking places at the center of American life; a period of strong economic recovery from the recession of the early '90s; markets carrying societies through transitions at which government has failed; a vision of computer-based grass-roots democracy . . . What the overarching American story line of the past thirty years is not about is a people and a political order equal, more than equal, to challenges and responsive to trumpet calls for reform; a society for whom successes, one upon another, have bred a shared national confidence, pride, motivation to meet the next challenge.

Good news is engaging. It encourages people to think inwardly as well as in participatory ways about the possibilities and opportunities occasioned by changes for the better. Bad news is the opposite.

And if its deeper meanings and emerging outline are cumulatively worse still — if the march of news portends societal, long-term economic and national decline, loss of human control of our destiny — it fosters not only alienation but depression. And if young people cannot see in such news enough to induce them to attend to it, the depression of adults translates into that much more deeply rooted disengagement on the part of the young.

And that is the heart of the dilemma with which the press has struggled. Considerations of new competition, revolutions in technology, challenges to business assumptions are all relevant. But the root of the matter is this: how to engage audiences for your basic product line — news — when the weight of so much from around the country and the world, over the length of one, going on two, generations, alienates and discourages them, or fails to impress them in any way at all? How to do so when, after so many decades of irresistible reasons and pressures to look outward, society turns so far inward in disengagement and so far into escapism for relief?

The choices available to the press in responding to the shift in cultural climate were limited the higher up the professional hierarchy you looked. As a medium of entertainment and visual delivery, television could, with some fluidity, adjust to mood: "featurize" itself; all you had to do was turn the machinery on. It could, in a harsher mode, offer the stylized perversity of "trash" or tabloid television; "talk radio" could appeal to people embittered and alienated by the drift of the news.

The problem for newspapers and their readers was more fundamental, for newspapers require the act of reading. The framing and writing and presentation of stories could all be made more entertaining, but only up to a point. If the newspaper wanted to hang on to its franchise as credible first drafter of history and "agenda setter," it had to worry more than television did about being taken seriously by opinion leaders and thoughtful readers.

The serious news media could not forever deny the essence of the disturbing new narrative. Millions of Americans from the 1930s through World War II and the postwar years and into the 1960s had felt part of the news and had seen their lives evolving in pace with the upward trajectory of American fortunes. But in the 1990s, as implied by front-page headlines like "Voters Disgusted with Politicians as Election Nears" (*The New York Times*, 1994) and "Many Americans View Washington as a Mess and Just Tune It Out" (*The Wall Street Journal*, 1997), denial of the news had become a form of existential logic.[3]

HAVING CONSIDERED THE cumulative pressures, trends, stresses, and events in the political and social spheres that pulled in the direction of disintegration, let us now look at the forces at work in the news business in the same time frame. This part of the story takes us into the particulars and peculiarities of that industry. But we engage along the way and wind up with the theme with which we started. That is, the interactivity of forces at work in the news business and in the public sphere, in politics, government, and society.

To begin with, in the 1960s and 1970s, managers of the news organizations were not of a mind to focus on the question of a mounting crisis in public consumption of their basic product, news. For within the industry, two other transforming processes were upsetting executives' standard operating procedures and consuming their time for strategic thinking. Each was to have a profound effect on the business, and on the country's system of communicating with itself.

THE FIRST TRANSITION at work was in the corporate structure of the news business.

The American press — the news business — evolves from an industry predominantly owned or controlled by founding entrepreneurs or resident members of family dynasties.

Several generational sequences converged in the news business in the 1960s and 1970s. Center stage, the founding fathers of the national press — the newsmagazines and television — were fading from the scene. Henry Luce, William Paley, David Sarnoff, and other media innovators lacked blood heirs up to the inheritance. Bureaucratization was inevitable.

To the side, but across the country and richer in tradition, many of the great newspapers were approaching their fourth or fifth generation of family ownership or control, and the great newspaper chains their second or third. Siblings and cousins, nephews and aunts, distant from the enterprise, were getting restless. Inheritance taxes were a problem. Merger and acquisition fever was on the rise. Command of news organizations' destiny depended on liquidity to buy out those restless relatives and counter the maneuvers of hungry dissidents among them. Money was needed as well to position the enterprise either aggressively or defensively in the quickening game of purchase and sale.

The corporate chains — Times Mirror, Gannett, Knight-Ridder — had begun buying up family-controlled local newspapers. To gain flexibility and develop their own growth positions, the stronger independent papers "went public," selling shares publicly for the first time. This step meant the family owners who went public had to make a choice over time.

In one scenario, a family could view its new liquidity as an instrument for preserving its "public service values" within a publicly owned corporation, focused clearly on the sustenance of a major newspaper property. Alternatively, an owning family could view that liquidity as an instrument with which to play the new corporate merger and acquisition game, either aggressively for the long term (to acquire), or for shorter-term profit (to be acquired). Acquiring new properties meant taking on debt; new revenue streams meant the ability to service that debt.

The Sulzbergers of *The New York Times* and the Grahams of *The Washington Post* were clear that they were choosing the first option. Their strategy, which included some acquisitions here and there, was not to become Times Mirror or Knight-Ridder. It was instead to secure a future for their flagship papers, among the foremost in the country and pride of the respective families, by building a corporate support system and revenue stream under them. And Sulzbergers and Grahams stayed at the corporate helms. By contrast, the McCormick and Chandler families vanished from the management of the *Chicago Tribune* and the *Los Angeles Times,* and the Gannetts from their chain. Those papers' parent companies went the other way, developing conglomerates based on the new corporate ethos, not the old family one.

In the middle were the families that owned the smaller franchises, the Cowleses of *The Minneapolis Tribune* and *Des Moines Register,* the Binghams of *The Louisville Courier-Journal,* the Taylors of *The Boston Globe,* who had trouble making up their minds which way to go. The owners felt conflicting pressures from relatives committed to "the family trust," relatives who were ready to cash in, and no end of financial advisers who could argue the case either way. Wrestling with those disparate interests, most of these second-rank owners wanted to honor the legacy of civic leadership and public trust, and also ride the value of their properties up in the boom market for newspapers. But their properties weren't big enough, their corporate positions weren't strong enough, their franchises weren't important or rich enough to enable them either to become acquirers, on the Times Mirror or Knight-Ridder plan, or "public trust" fortresses on the Graham or Sulzberger plan. One by one from the mid-1980s on, many of them roiled in ambivalence or intramural conflict, these owners sold the family jewels to chains or larger papers.[4]

FOR A TIME, though, the prospects were dazzling either way, even for those owners ambivalent about the question whether ultimately they held on or sold. For "going public" generated welcome cash reserves, and it eased the families' inheritance tax problems.

Within the news business in the same time frame, computerization was cutting costs radically by eliminating whole categories of machines and labor. By 1990, newspaper production workforces and labor costs were roughly half what they had been in the 1960s and 1970s, and profitability had doubled, from profit margins under 10 percent to levels approaching 20 percent.[5]

Computerization drove other elements of the news business boom. Its impact on industry in all fields and the emergence of a new computer industry itself prompted transformations in the labor force. There were new jobs for those who could handle computers; early retirement, buyouts, and the thriving part-time job market for others. In larger metropolitan markets, the result was a tremendous boom for newspaper "help wanted" classified advertising, and other uses of classifieds by those taking the buyouts and moving on — trading in the old family house for a retirement home, for example. And the electronic makeover paid a handsome dividend: with computers, newspapers could handle classified advertising in volume with a speed and efficiency impossible in times past, with the prospect of eliminating their "ad taker" workforce (rife with featherbedding) in new labor contracts. Thus computerization meant enormous labor and production savings for newspapers in their own operations, and a bonanza at the other end of the labor market, in cost-efficient classified ads.[6]

Looking outward from the business, society was on the edge of an "information revolution," also thanks to the computer. The revolution included scenarios for the convergence of print and electronic media formats, exploration of the frontiers of consumer interactivity, instant consumer access to all sorts of background information and data, "synergy" among news, information, and entertainment media. In news business front offices, "future shock" meant exciting opportunities for enterprise.

THRIVING, DIVERSIFYING, CHARTING new markets, the news business in the 1970s became a formidable player in the economy. It even met, and bested, the power of the state, going the other way.

Infuriated by dissident former Defense Department analyst Daniel Ellsberg's leaking of the Pentagon Papers to *The New York Times* in June 1971, the Nixon administration obtained a court injunction to stop the newspaper from publishing the documents. The *Times* appealed, and while the case moved up to the Supreme Court, Ellsberg passed another copy of the Pentagon Papers to *The Washington Post*.

By an accident of timing, these events played out the very week that *The Washington Post* was scheduled to go public. Owner-publisher Katharine Graham's business managers and lawyers pleaded with her not to feed the fire and imperil the public offering of *Post* shares by lining up alongside *The New York Times* in defiance of the Nixon administration. There could be (warned the advisers) immediate legal repercussions that would undermine the public stock offering, and beyond that, revenge by the Nixon administration on the *Post*. The Post Company's cash cow was CBS's Washington television affiliate, WTOP, and there had been rumblings from Nixon's heavies about organizing challenges to the *Post*'s ownership of it before the Federal Communications Commission.

Graham faced down her cautious counselors and published the next installments of the Pentagon Papers. The *Post*'s public offering went forward. The Supreme Court's next step was a 6–3 ruling for the press and against the Nixon administration, reinforcing its 1964 articulation of press prerogatives in *Times v. Sullivan*. Graham's next step was to fire her lawyers and hire a bolder team.[7]

FOR THE SHORT term, a number of trends in the news business worked to reinforce one another. The computer was enabling the news business to operate at once more efficiently and more expansively. Labor costs were falling. The surge of television into the media marketplace, together with demographic and workforce trends, forced the elimination of weaker big-city newspapers from the competition, particularly in the afternoon field. The stronger papers, having enjoyed dominance in their markets, became real or virtual monopolies. Another beneficiary was the suburban daily, frequently an afternoon paper oriented to local news, a supplement rather than a competitive threat to the major metropolitan dailies.

Many of these dominant or monopoly players in the metropolitan markets — in cities including Los Angeles, Chicago, Miami, Philadelphia, Atlanta, Baltimore, Des Moines, Louisville, Houston, Hartford — were anchors or links in the major newspaper chains, or fated to be purchased by them. In past decades, noted Gene Roberts, executive editor of Knight-Ridder's *Philadelphia Inquirer* in the 1970s and 1980s, "There were chains, Hearst and Scripps-Howard, but they were usually the second and third papers in multipaper cities. What is new . . . is the growth of newspaper companies whose primary holdings are in monopoly markets." Add the new monopoly positions to crisply managed chain ownership at Knight-Ridder, Times Mirror, Gannett, and the lesser chains, and you had a recipe for the generation of enormous profits. News business fortunes soared. Media stocks took off. Wall Street loved them. The sky was the limit.[8]

However: the owners of news organizations did not know it in the

1970s, but in locking the new corporate imperative onto their businesses they were inviting the gradual loss of control of their destinies to alien forces — Wall Street analysts and traders, merger and acquisition entrepreneurs, "the market," "the bottom line." Nor could these suddenly lionized "media industry" executives imagine what would happen to the basic commodity in which they traded, news.

A DECADE LATER, a second wave of change rolled out in the media marketplace.

Computerization and shifting demographics fuel a revolution in the techniques of advertising and marketing.

A trademark of strong newspapers had long been the volume of advertising — roughly 50 percent of newspaper ad revenue — from the department stores that served as landmarks in a given city: Macy's and Gimbel's in New York, Jordan Marsh and Filene's in Boston, Hecht's and Woodward & Lothrop in Washington, Marshall Field's in Chicago, and so on across the country. As industry analyst Leo Bogart put it, "Those stores ran ads day in and day out, beefing up daily newspaper bulk and adding to reader appeal. The ads reflected the freshness and immediacy of the stores' tactical merchandising decisions; they were newsworthy."[9]

By the 1970s, many newspapers, especially those that had lately achieved dominance or monopoly status, had grown accustomed to the point of arrogance about automatic advertising rate increases for these and other prominent, long-term retailers. These rate increases fueled the papers' phenomenal revenue growth. But the same technological advances that were spurring newspapers on began to offer retail advertisers the weapons of rebellion.

As newspapers, with the help of computerization, began to be able to zone themselves more precisely in the 1970s and 1980s, retailers began to demand access to readers according to zip codes and other delivery routes, zoned for impact. The papers themselves were raising their ad rates, but they had only limited capabilities for color and zoning. Enter "preprints," those stand-alone color advertising supplements hawking bargains and sales, inserted into the Sunday and sometimes the daily paper.

Ominously for newspapers, as Bogart noted, advertisers were opting for their own zoned marketing strategies, as distinct from their longtime dependence on newspaper formats. Between 1976 and 1986 advertisers' expenditures for preprints soared from $835 million to $4.1 *billion* — a 400 percent increase. (By 1997 the figure was $12.6 billion.)

As with age to the body, newspapers lost something of their muscular appearance as preprints took hold, while accumulating excess clutter in fat Sunday editions. Publishers hated preprints, pulling as they did from "run of paper" (ROP) placement of ads, integrated with news and features. But they could hardly afford to say goodbye to the advertising revenue at stake. So they suffered preprints and tried to fight them, raising rates for them in the hope of driving retailers back to ROP advertising. Instead, that move pushed many retailers, especially grocery stores, out of newspapers for good.

The advertisers' embrace of preprints was not a friendly move and not the last, thanks to the emergence of direct mail techniques. A cheap one (taken up by the grocery and drug chains) enabled advertisers to contract directly with the U.S. Postal Service to saturate homes and mailboxes with preprints; farewell to the newspaper as carrier.

Sophisticated retailers found more finely honed tools. Gradually it became possible for them to compile electronic databases on their own and send handsome catalogs to customers targeted demographically and by taste and buying habits. By these means they could, in addition, achieve a much more measurable response for each advertising dollar spent than with the old mass market approach.[10]

THE NEW TECHNIQUES came together under the heading of direct marketing. They reflected a fundamental shift in advertising theory and practice — slow to take form but accelerating — from the mass marketing to the "targeted" approach.

In fact, the marketers' analyses reflected the political and cultural trends of the times, and paralleled the observations of political consultants and their candidates. The issue for the advertising and marketing industries was not simply refinement of technique, said their seers. It was as well the transformation of American society and culture from the unity of World War II, and the postwar model of a swelling middle-class reflecting growing commonality, to a fragmented one.

Commentators in the authoritative trade magazine *Advertising Age* saw the nation as "less homogeneous, more splintered" as a consequence of racial tensions and the Vietnam War, and "split asunder into innumerable special interests — gray power, gay power, red power, black power, Sunbelt and frostbelt, environmentalists and industrialists . . . all more aware of their claims on society." This tended to be a coldly analytic judgment rather than a normative one; on the other hand, Rance Crain, the magazine's publisher, wrote in late 1984 that a lesson of Reagan's reelection that year was that the public was "tired of making sacrifices."[11]

Marketers had been alert early on to the emergence of the baby boom generation. They noted its penchant for "questioning traditional values and ways of life" and interest in "the search for their own identities and new types of communities," wrote media historian Joseph Turow.

"To many ad executives such changes reflected a society with increasingly divided interests," Turow argued, " 'a public moving to its own drumbeat,' " more "fractured and income-polarized," more "self-indulgent," living at an "increasingly frenetic" pace. Such observations, parallel to those that were beginning to trouble political and social thinkers, spelled something more like delicious opportunity to marketers: "At the start of the '80s [marketing] executives forecast that the decade would mark, in the words of one, 'a continuing trend away from the Protestant ethic . . . and toward self-fulfillment.' The nation would see the proliferation of a 'me-first' mentality. There would be a greater concern with pleasure and money as a 'tool for pleasure.' "

The frustration for advertisers and marketers, Turow added, was that major media — newspapers, general interest magazines, network television — were still so oriented to the traditional mass market philosophy. Thus, "the 1980s marked an odd period . . . when marketers' use of media to reach Americans did not match their own sense of the fragmenting of American life or their methods for searching out the fragments."[12]

In such a volatile marketplace, the advent of the new direct marketing techniques had multiple effects. Newspapers struggled for ways to turn them to advantage, building their own subscriber databases and working to entice retailers into collaborative use of these devices. Some retailers flaunted their new independence and newspapers' new weakness: "Newspapers have to realize that the automatic 4–7 percent [ad rate] increase every year is not going to happen unless there's a 4 to 7 percent circulation base gain," a department store executive told the publishers' trade journal, *Presstime*. But circulation was flat or falling, and newspaper industry executives who used to call the shots for advertisers were playing a poor defensive game.

Industry analyst John Morton ridiculed the clumsiness of some measures newspapers felt forced to take to accommodate retailers in search of target marketing, such as their "own foray into junk mail," and "into investing many millions of dollars in inserting machines and other equipment required to compete." Some papers, wrote Morton, went so far as "to offer advertisers delivery of [preprint] circulars by mail to homes that don't receive newspapers."[13]

Meanwhile the papers' old, lately fickle friends, the big-city department stores, were developing glossy catalogs for direct mail use. But the big-city department stores, like big cities themselves, were in trouble.

For onto the retailing battlefield marched the Gap, the Limited, Banana Republic, and all the fixtures of the mall, offering impatient customers on wheels convenience, a focused shopping environment, and trendy "designer" products that erased class lines. These exponents of consumer self-fulfillment were joined by the efficient discounters, led by Wal-Mart. The "baby boom" retailers blended the old mail-order catalog and new computer-driven targeting tools, yielding a supple instrument for reaching consumers without reference to or dependence on such media as newspapers or magazines (though "image ads" on television were often part of the formula). Meanwhile, like so many dinosaurs, the landmark department stores were headed for junk-bond-financed consolidations, and a number of them from there into bankruptcy.

Into the homes of readers, along with preprints, came reams of sleekly designed, demographically targeted catalogs with messages of affordable upmarket chic, uninterrupted by downbeat news. Climbing out of the phone came the kudzu of telemarketing. Expenditures on direct mail, about $5 billion in the mid-1970s, began a steady surge; they were almost $40 billion by 1998. Telemarketing expenditures were $34 billion in the mid-1980s, $73 billion a decade later. Catalog companies sent out 7 billion pieces of direct mail in 1980, 14 billion in 1990. An American Newspaper Publishers Association team coined a new term for the phenomenon: "bypass," as in bypassing the news media middleman.[14]

Easing the newspaper industry's "bypass" pain for the short run was the fact that the classified advertising boom more than offset the retail advertising losses. But contemplation of the big picture, had the news industry's top executives engaged in it, could offer little comfort.

For societal, cultural, and political fragmentation fed both the sense that "news" in broad, shared terms was irrelevant and the new marketplace gospel, awkward at best for the news business to adapt to, that targeted audiences counted for more than mass audiences. The combination of these trends would hurt the news business coming and going.

BY 1990, THE trajectories of the several trends at work were beginning to cross. The peak year for newspaper circulation growth, 1973, had also been the high point in recent decades for newspapers' share of total U.S. advertising volume (29.9 percent, as against 17.9 percent for television and 14.8 percent for direct mail; in 1997 those numbers stood at 22.1 percent for newspapers and 19.7 percent each for television and direct mail).

Advertising revenue for newspapers, a constantly rising figure year by year with only brief pauses during recessions like the one in 1957–58, hit a wall in the recession year 1989, recovering significantly only by 1994. But through that dark half-decade for the newspaper business, total direct mail revenues never faltered, and television revenues slipped for one year only (1991).[15]

Meanwhile, the high prices paid for newspaper acquisitions in the 1980s had to be justified by high profits in the 1990s. Sizable debt burdens for the acquisitions had to be financed. At chains like Gannett and Capital Cities that meant a more or less candid policy of milking the papers and broadcast properties — cutting costs, investing little or nothing in them, raising circulation and ad rates to the limit — to service the debt. The gamble was that management along such lines would maintain profit margin growth.

Even for healthy newspapers profiting from the consolidation of the marketplace down to one or two newspapers per city, the seemingly limitless expansion of the 1960s and 1970s was coming to a halt. James Squires claims that his reputation in the eyes of the Tribune Company executives who brought him from their top second-string paper to the editorship of the *Chicago Tribune* in 1981 was based on his "ability to produce increasingly respectable newspapers on the cheap, more profitable each year than the last, without requiring additional resources." But by the time he left the *Tribune* in bitter circumstances in 1989, he writes, he and other managers at the paper were annually "called on to do more with less, while the demand for increasing profits never ceased. I had become a smoke-and-mirrors magician, juggling from the right hand to the left, robbing Peter to pay Paul and lying to myself and my staff about how successful we were. Enough would never be enough."[16]

FOR HELP, NEWSPAPERS began to turn to a cluster of industry consultants. At *The Boston Globe* in the late 1970s and early 1980s, the publisher periodically summoned mid-level and senior editors along with circulation, advertising, and marketing department managers for presentations by some of these consultants, including the late, influential Ruth Clark.

On the surface their findings, always supported by survey and focus group findings, charts, and slides, were thoughtful. The competition for readers, the message went, was no longer the other paper in town, the feisty tabloid "up the street," but television and "people's time." Television increasingly controlled the market for breaking news, but newspapers "set the agenda" for television. The demographic and behavioral patterns of the country were changing dramatically: proliferation beyond the suburbs of exurban living and shopping, new definitions of leisure, women in the workplace, concern for fitness.

Our "product," we were told, was of high quality. We had all the credentials for being reckoned the city's and the region's "paper of record," and one of the ten or twelve best papers in the country. We sported our badges of distinction: our national and foreign news bureaus, our string of Pulitzer Prizes, our popular columnists, some of them syndicated. Everyone loved our sportswriters; some of our reporters in technical fields were sharp. We "owned" the affluent suburbs as to circulation; we reaped the lion's share of advertising in our market as a result. The tabloid *Boston Herald* couldn't touch us, except on city news. Our penetration of the metropolitan market (that is, the percentage of the households in it we reached) was weak—it hovered around 33 percent—owing to the hold of the afternoon dailies in the ring of old, small cities circling Boston. That was a cause for concern, but not a threat.

But readers complained of the volume of bad and tedious news in the paper, stories about chicanery, crime, governmental process. And there was the public perception of us as "biased," according to one viewpoint or another.

The *Globe* had "got in front of its readers," in the words of J. Anthony Lukas, with its fervent support of the court-ordered school busing plan that tore Boston apart in the 1970s. Irish-American working-class bitterness toward the WASP Yankee-owned and edited paper was an issue thereafter. The *Globe*'s efforts to compensate for that bitterness often came across as awkward or staged, and the net result rendered us not (as was hoped) balanced, but uneven and sometimes cacophonous.

The *Globe* tried to appease Boston's white working class, among other ways with decades of tolerance of columnist Mike Barnicle's "bad boy" antics (though Barnicle lived handsomely in the comfortable western suburbs, he positioned himself as the voice of Irish South Boston's disenfranchised). At the same time, working from a mold fixed in the feisty 1960s, the paper's sharply liberal editorial page was echoed by favored reporters who behaved like, or doubled as, unbuttoned columnists pushing a McGovern-liberal point of view. That was not exactly the view of white working-class residents of "Southie"—or of readers of all stripes who found such content self-indulgent. By the 1980s, many of the *Globe*'s readers and a number of its reporters and editors agreed that its proud reputation as Boston's "paper of record" was at odds with the "biased" and "uneven" labels attaching to it. So there was reason to entertain the consultants' refrain that if we wanted to continue to thrive, we needed to understand our post-1960s readers' tastes better.[17]

These were not occasions for finger-pointing by the business managers at the incorrigible newsroom and editorial board. They instead passed as times for reflection, for acknowledgment that "we're all in it together," along with the rest of the newspaper industry. The business side heard the part about the paper's franchise on quality in the local marketplace and respected it. Sometimes these sessions included presentations around new sets of tools for understanding contemporary society: market research analyses of the dawning age, much more au courant than the clunky rundowns of old based on obvious educational, class, ethnic, income, employment, or residential statistics. One was the Stanford Research Institute's VALS (Values and Life Styles) study, a "psychographic" exercise in "slicing and dicing" (so went the trade talk) metropolitan markets into tribal categories like *outer-* and *inner-directed consumers,* and subcategories like *survivors, sustainers, belongers, emulators,* and *achievers.* (A similar study's socioeconomic handles included *bohemian mix, blue-blood estates,* and *shotguns and pick-ups.*)[18]

A film of short-take interviews with representatives of the VALS subcultures accompanied discussion and handouts. I recall a segment on an *achiever* or "newly leisured" couple, blue-collar according to old reckonings, lounging in their new home hot tub with champagne glasses, reflecting with satisfaction on their lifestyle values; food for thought.

The first customers for these forms of market research were from the ranks of advertising, circulation, and promotion. But the idea, we understood and could at least consider, was to take this evolving social portrait of democratic America to heart in editing the newspaper as well as marketing it. This message we reflected upon in various purposeful as well as ironic ways. Of a late afternoon or evening in the newsroom, you could hear the sardonic copy-desk honcho erupting midway through yet another long, dutiful, detailed report on some governmental wrangle: "BO-ring!"

Reflecting on the sessions with the consultants, reflecting on what was meant by "BO-ring," it was not hard to feel a member of the fabled assembly of the blind trying to identify the strange animal in our midst, divining the nature of the beast on the basis of limited and superficial sensations. A hand to the elephant's flank: "Yes, very like a horse."

THE MESSAGES, in fact, were the merest skim from deep currents flowing in the nation. There was nothing profound in their findings. The "psychographics" scheme was merely the stuff of an advertising sales campaign, not of research mining the studies of history, sociology, psychology, economics, or political science.[19]

At issue was not the merit of polling and focus group research to assist in thoughtful decision making. At issue was the application of the findings. Politicians were buying such research in order to get, and stay, elected. News executives were learning to do something quite like that. In both cases, however, the effect was to pull away from thoughtful decision making and toward mechanical reflexes. Put aside self-generated insights, assessments, instincts for leadership (went the new line). "Manage" the problem, based on assessment of public likes and dislikes.

To an industry in the business of discovering and interpreting news, an industry knocked off its stride by developments and confused by their effects, came not insight into the deeper currents flowing in society but the reflex of going with that flow. There was no consideration of the possibility that we might be looking at trouble rather deeper than what the industry consultants were talking about.

Would it have been possible to suggest in such a session — elaborate clearing of the throat, disclaimers, and so forth — that we might in fact be facing the premature end of "the American Century," or a crisis of the modern spirit? In a business so driven by its own linear past and by the gritty here and now, it would have been as inappropriate a leap as a suggestion that we take off our clothes and get in touch with our feelings.

Instead, as fear about flat circulation and low reader interest began to intensify, the wagons were drawn closer, and the managers of the news business talked principally to one another. Raw research on

the editorial side consisted of the closely held focus group transcripts and survey statistics. Expertise consisted of the obvious extrapolations from them. Publishers and top editors took their buzzword solutions to the disturbing trends from the language of advertising and technology: "consumer-driven," "customer obsession," "interactivity," "targeting," "branding," "relationship marketing."
The owners and managers of the news business were on the edge of becoming at once the desperate authors and confused consumers of their own superficial strategy for getting by in an ominously transformed social and political environment.

AND YET IN the first years of alarm about adverse trends for the news business, the bottom line held, or could be held, in firm enough check. Readership was down — but higher circulation pricing was maintaining revenue. Retail advertising was significantly down — but classified advertising was mopping up the losses. Costs were down, thanks to automation, and computerization promised further streamlining of operations from the newsroom to the circulation department.
On balance, profits and profit margins were up for the newspaper industry through the 1970s and 1980s. That meant the slippage could be put "in perspective," if not outright denied. In "going public" in the 1970s, the industry adopted the corporate bottom-line imperative. For a while the bottom line protected it from its own worst fears.

EIGHT

Managing

FOR THE MEN and women who manage the press, the onset of the industry crisis in the late 1980s came in rough, cross-cutting waves, packing undertow. How exactly to characterize the pounding effect was difficult, because "the crisis" was in fact a convergence of crises. Industry leaders and analysts tended to focus on one or another aspect of them, with results that variously reflected superficiality, distraction, and confusion.

The first waves, in the 1980s, were the consequences of privately held companies going public and of merger and acquisition fever in the go-go years. For a publicly traded corporation to maintain its glow in the eyes of Wall Street analysts, annual profitability had to grow — even in bad years. Maintaining profitability was not a grave challenge in the late 1970s and the 1980s, as new technologies enabled the press to realize vast savings in labor and production. In the newspaper field, the death of weaker newspapers was strengthening the position of the survivors. But matching past performance became a problem for all news media as circulation, readership, and television news viewership went flat in the 1980s, and then into decline, and as the direct marketing revolution began to cut into advertising in the 1990s.[1]

To a profit-driven media corporation looking for growth, an independently controlled newspaper was potentially an attractive purchase. These papers generally suffered from internal tensions over the future of ownership that played into the hands of buyers. They were usually ripe for cost cutting, and lagging in efforts to make the most of their market positions. And so the remaining independently owned papers became the subject of endless speculation as to whether or not they were "in play" as acquisition targets, or about to be.

That was the situation in the 1980s at *The Boston Globe,* as at the Field family's *Chicago Sun-Times,* the Cowles family's papers in Minneapolis and Des Moines, the Bingham family's *Louisville Courier-Journal,* and others. It was an alien specter that moved in and out of view, demanding attention, permitting denial.[2]

By the late 1980s, the convergence of the adverse forces was deepening the standard tensions between newsrooms and their front-office management. At *The Philadelphia Inquirer,* the most prestigious paper in the Knight-Ridder chain, differences between an unusually strong editor (Eugene L. Roberts) and a corporate executive destined for the CEO position (Anthony P. Ridder, one of the last members of an owning family in chain management) served as a test case of what was happening throughout the industry.

Gene Roberts represented journalistic enterprise of the first order, as evidenced by the *Inquirer's* seventeen Pulitzer Prizes during the years of his editorship. At the end of the 1980s *Inquirer* profit margins were rising but still below the level corporate headquarters had set, so Roberts faced pressure to curtail his news operations. After "brass-knuckle, white knuckle" arguments in 1989 over the next year's budget, "a hell of a battle" closely watched by others in the industry, Roberts claimed to "feel extremely good" about the results. But satisfaction proved fleeting, for bad times were coming. And as *The New York Times* noted, the corporation's Tony Ridder "insists that profit margins be maintained" — that is, in bad times as well as good.[3]

For decades, top editors, business managers, and owners of many news organizations had collaborated on the cultivation of their properties with mutual understanding of cyclical ups and downs, and relatively little other outside inhibition or pressure. There was common cause too in protecting the franchise during hard times, accepting lower profits or even losses, and reinvesting in the business during good times. The long haul included raising prices, and strong papers therefore worked to "give back" to the reader and advertiser with periodic special features, enhancement of the news and editorial content of the paper, new equipment to improve its presentation and delivery. But the corporatization of the news business imposed another, external agenda altogether: a schedule of profitability according to Wall Street stock market analysts' measurements and timetables.[4]

That put friction and divergence of interest of the kind *The Philadelphia Inquirer* experienced into the news business, front and center. Front-office managers, no longer merely collaborators with their top editors, were still only beginning to push against the walls that protected the newsroom from marketing imperatives. But they were imposing more and more budget and performance direction on their newsrooms, and more willful interference overall—a willfulness driven by insecurity. This was especially pronounced in the large newspaper chains, where the task was to make the broadest grids of numbers come out on target. By the end of 1989 two respected top editors—Bill Kovach of the Cox papers' flagship, *The Atlanta Journal-Constitution,* and Jim Squires of the Tribune Company's flagship *Chicago Tribune*—had left their jobs as a consequence. Knight-Ridder's Gene Roberts followed, leaving *The Philadelphia Inquirer* in 1990.[5] (For a word on my own, earlier departure as editor of *The Boston Globe,* see note 5.)

ALL THAT WAS mild sparring compared with what happened next: the recession of the late 1980s and early 1990s. In 1990, total advertising sales for the newspaper industry fell for the first time in twenty years. Newspapers threw out their advertising "rate cards" and negotiated what deals they could. Reports noted shocking falloffs in daily readership: for example, from 75 percent of people between ages thirty and forty-four, in 1972, to 45 percent in 1989. Alex Jones of *The New York Times* reported 1991 to have been "a year the industry considers the worst in half a century."[6]

Nevertheless the new corporate rules about profitability and bottom-line performance held firm. No more rolling with the cyclical punch; the order of the day was to hold to "plan"—that is, profit targets. That meant, among other measures, stringent retrenchment of news and editorial operations, one of the only "soft" places left for cost cutting. "What if by March you are 2 percent under plan or

5 percent under plan?" asked Squires with rhetorical ire in the wake of his departure from the *Chicago Tribune.* "You don't ever adjust the profit and say we're not going to make as much. You adjust the cost and say we're still going to make as much."[7]

Moreover the decline and death of second and third newspapers in most cities, at first an unmitigated boon to the dominant or monopoly survivors, yielded problematical side effects as well. Competition had been a never ending trigger of reader interest. People had been able to find one paper closer to their tastes than the other, or to change their minds and switch. But editorially, the paper left holding the field had to be all things to all people. As the only newspaper show in town it became a more visible target for resentment of its power. And on the business side, much, much more in the way of bottom-line performance was expected of a strongly dominant or monopoly property than one engaged in fierce competition.

NEWSPAPERS MOVED TO unload their "unprofitable" circulation. In the depths of the recession of the early 1990s *The Des Moines Register,* a Gannett purchase in 1985, abandoned its long-standing commitment to circulate across the state of Iowa. *The Los Angeles Times* eliminated editions for whole regions in its vast circulation range. Simply raising circulation and advertising prices eliminated less affluent readers and marginal advertisers, and helped the bottom line.

Such moves revealed "the dirty little secret of newspapering," wrote Squires in 1993, the more so given the industry's cries of gloom and doom: "a business that has always claimed to rest on a public trust" depends for its "highest profitability . . . [on] delivering advertising sold at the highest rates in a paper containing the fewest pages and sold for the highest possible retail price to the fewest high-income customers necessary to justify the highest rate to advertisers."[8]

Squires, the only veteran of the news business wars to write a critical book about them, was as bitter as a shrewd and able newsman could be at the collapse of what he frankly called the complex bargain he'd struck with the *Tribune*'s corporate command. His analysis, however, left out the issue of audience alienation — as distinct from news organizations' elimination of slices of the audience.

A perspective that saw the whole picture clearly was hard to come by, and distracted by contradictory predictions for what was coming next.

Nervous rather than strategically organized, those in command of the news business through the 1990s flew like geese from one to another assertion of the scope and nub of the problem. And so interviews and industry convention proceedings produced a flow of conflicting diagnoses: We're in a cyclical recession; no big deal . . . Wrong, we're undergoing systemic, structural change and it's a very big, very bad deal . . . The real issue is television's negative impact on readership . . . Wrong; it's new competition for advertising . . . No, it's failure to come to terms with "new media" technology . . . Wrong, in a fragmented marketplace it's failure to make direct contact with readers and viewers, whom we must learn to call "customers."

"Publishers Look Hard at Content of Papers," read the headline on a *New York Times* dispatch from the 1994 publishers' convention reporting yet another flight of the geese. "After years of blaming things like declining literacy rates and increasing competition from television for the problems of American newspapers," the *Times* reported,

> the publishers of the country's big dailies have turned to a new culprit: their own publications. . . . The new industry focus on news content comes after several years of anxiety about declines in advertising and what some publishers say has been a consuming focus on new technologies for information delivery. . . .
>
> There was no dissent . . . when Tom Peters, the management consultant, [told the publishers] "The truth is . . . the average newspaper in the average city I go to bores the living daylights out of me."[9]

THE CORPORATE CHIEFTAINS of the news business were confounded by its dilemmas, and they flailed around for solutions. The reports on the state of the industry quoted top managers looking grimly on the bright side: "Nothing focuses your attention like pain"; the downturn was a "blessing in disguise" that "snapped the industry out of its torpor" and made news organizations "look very hard at other ways of generating revenues." The talk, noted *Newsweek,* was of "spiffy graphics and splashy colors," of redesign according to the *USA Today* model and 900 numbers for updates on listings, of new themed sections aimed at the MTV generation . . . and of budget reductions, staff layoffs, and buyouts.[10]

"How people [in the news business] respond to trouble depends on who they are," remarked John Morton wryly. He meant that those, like the Sulzbergers and Grahams, who had decided early on that in going public they were reinforcing the family newspaper franchise and were only secondarily in the merger and acquisition game, were more secure in the face of marketplace adversity than those who managed the large chains and media conglomerates. The latter were more totally creatures of corporate culture than the New York Times Company or Washington Post Company. The chain executives were more susceptible to the whim and will of outside directors and Wall Street; job security and "executive compensation packages" in those conglomerates were more directly reflective of the price of the company's stock than at corporations still honoring "the family trust."[11]

The late James Batten, CEO of Knight-Ridder, the chain that published such standout papers as *The Miami Herald,* the *San Jose Mercury News,* and the *Detroit Free Press,* along with *The Philadelphia Inquirer,* was one of the most thoughtful news business proprietors of the 1980s and 1990s. Batten's trumpeting of the "customer obsession" gospel irritated some reporters and editors, but having distinguished himself first in the newsroom, he was in fact one of the most journalistically committed industry executives to be found. Yet even he could seem at sea.

"Call them customers or call them readers, we don't have enough of them," Batten told *The Wall Street Journal* as Knight-Ridder launched its "Project 25/43," an effort to attract baby boomer readers between the demographically attractive ages of twenty-five and forty-three with "reader-friendly" editing, light on weighty content, heavy on graphics. "We have to try something."[12]

Less fortunate in his choice of rhetoric was Mark Willes, a vice chairman of General Mills recruited in 1995 by the troubled Times Mirror Corporation, owner of properties including *The Los Angeles Times, Newsday, The Baltimore Sun,* and *The Hartford Courant.* A proud, expansion-minded industry leader in the 1970s and 1980s, Times Mirror's management was under heavy fire from Wall Street for its troubled financial performance and decision making in the marketplace fallout of the 1990s. In plucking Willes from the packaged-food business, Times Mirror passed over two carefully trained heirs apparent on its management team.

Praising his new employer's "brand franchises," Willes, known as a cost cutter, stressed financial imperatives. He told Bill Glaberson of *The New York Times* shortly after his arrival at Times Mirror, " 'If you're not the low-cost producer, you're not going to have the kinds of margins you need to work with' to assure investors an adequate return." Warming to his theme, the confident Willes described his plans to apply lessons from the packaged-goods industry to the newspaper business; "newspapers needed to 'refresh' what they offer readers regularly," he said, "just as consumer-products companies regularly improve products." What had he in mind as a comparison, asked Glaberson. Why, "the successful marketing of cereals, Hamburger Helper and cake mixes," Willes obliged. That settled the question of Willes's nickname as he proceeded on a course of radical retrenchment at Times Mirror, including the elimination of 3,000 jobs (140 in *The Los Angeles Times*'s news staff alone) and the closing of *Newsday*'s spinoff, *New York Newsday:* "the cereal killer."[13]

Willes embarked on what he was happy to have described in the press as "shock treatment," a year of "the most arduous downsizing and cost-cutting the industry has ever seen." In the summer of 1996, a year into his tenure at Times Mirror, Willes found himself repeatedly pressed for his plan for the company's growth following recovery. He acknowledged that "so many people are frustrated with me": "They say, 'How are you gonna grow it,' and I say, 'I don't know.' "[14]

Batten and Willes ran the two premier media chains in the country. They led an industry with a committed base in dominant, top-quality, big-city newspapers, with millions of dollars invested in "communications revolution" research and experimentation, and in strategic positioning in other media. Between them, the two CEOs

were informed, tough-minded representatives of the two traditional components of the news business: *news* (Batten) and *business*
(Willes).

If what these two leaders could offer in the way of strategic analysis and vision was so limited, the quality of intellectual leadership
elsewhere in the news business could not be expected to be incisive.
By 1995, Batten was dead of a brain tumor at fifty-nine. By 1997,
as we shall see, Willes had found himself a plan that rocked and
shocked the industry as well as the journalism profession.

ELSEWHERE IN THE news business, conditions were no better. The
newsmagazines were holding on to their mass market numbers, but
only at the high price of acquisition of new, cut-rate subscriptions to
replace those lost. The recession cut into their ad revenues and ability to hold to their stated ad rates; they began to accept "adver-
torials" and other intrusive arrangements on advertisers' terms. The
newsmagazines tried redesigning themselves and having their week-
in, week-out staffs move over for "name" writers. They cut back on
their far-flung bureaus and reporting staffs, downplayed foreign and
national news, and pushed entertainment, celebrities, and lifestyle
trends. Having done so, the wiser heads running them acknowledged that their largest problem was identity crisis. (They tended not
to acknowledge that much of it was self-inflicted.)[15]

In 1997 *Time*, which had slashed its roster of correspondents and
reporters almost in half from the early 1980s to the mid-1990s, ran
one foreign news cover (not counting its two in a row on the death of
Princess Diana); in 1987 it had run eleven. *Newsweek* and *Time*,
whose calling cards had once been a depth of hard-news coverage
most newspapers couldn't hope to match, picked such cover subjects
in the late '90s as JonBenet Ramsey, Brad Pitt, Versace, asthma, and
fat. (Worried about the aging of their subscribers, they instructed
their arts critics to focus on entertainment popular with the young.
But why in the world of the '90s would fans of funkier new sounds
turn to *Time* or *Newsweek* when newsstands were bulging with
magazines niched precisely to them?)[16]

Thus transformed, the newsmagazines became vulnerable to the
dread disease of lesser media: publication of underreported hype

and fraud. In 1998, *Time* embarrassed itself in its unfortunate "synergy" with corporate cousin CNN by reporting the alleged use of nerve gas against American deserters in Vietnam as fact, and members of the *Newsweek* staff were notable among those engaged in overeager coverage of Monica Lewinsky's turn on the national wheel of fortune.[17]

The fate of the television news divisions was ever more hostage to the fragmentation of the networks' overall position and the wholly market-driven priorities of parent companies including Disney, Time Warner, and General Electric. In 1994, CBS, ABC, NBC, and Fox controlled 68 percent of prime-time television audiences. By 1998, with soaring costs of sure-fire sports and entertainment packages wiping out profits, that figure had fallen below 60 percent for the first time ever. Amid CBS executives' denials of doomsday rumors that year that the network was contemplating shutting down its news-gathering operations, a *New York Times* report stated flatly, "CBS cannot compete with CNN, MSNBC and the Fox News Channel in the 24-hour news business. Nor can ABC and NBC."

"We used to think the possibility existed that erosion was going to stop," said the president of ABC, Robert Iger. "We were silly. It's never going to stop. As you give consumers greater and greater choices, they are going to make more choices. . . . If the economics don't change significantly, it just won't work anymore."

The once mighty NBC and CBS were routinely said to be heading for sale, but they were also described as overpriced. More recent entrants to the broadcast field "have proven they can launch their own networks for far less money," an industry expert observed.[18]

SO MANY OF the received truths about the news business went up in smoke so fast that the industry, accustomed to charts and graphs depicting steady upward trend lines, had trouble assimilating the news. "Future shock," replete with technological and marketplace as well as social and economic impact, was "now shock." Meanwhile, the forces at the gates were hungry, impatient, and indifferent if not hostile to traditional news business values. These were the information-age "highwaymen" (in Ken Auletta's phrasing) and "Darth Vaders" (in Al Gore's): Rupert Murdoch, John Malone, Bill

Gates, and the others, wielding "life and death power" in their struggles "to crush competitors and . . . take the risks out of capitalism."[19]

The news business had always been both highly immediate and
present in American life, in clear-cut ways: as news courier, and as
parapolitical opinion leader. In the 1990s, with the fragmentation of
the media and political environments, the press saw itself whittled
back on both scores. Riddles about the new technologies impeded
cogent thinking about the future. Just how technologically oriented,
how cyberspaced, did society want to be? Computer-age gurus' predictions were guarantees of little. Their claims as to how the multi-
tudes would take to the latest technologies were as spotty as those at
previous threshold moments when research and development passed
to the marketplace. But news business executives plunged forward
anyway, with more mixed results. Tony Ridder spoke of his company's "evolution from print to a full-service information provider,"
but it was Knight-Ridder that had lost an estimated $50 million on
premature marketing of an early, inefficient "electronic newspaper"
system, Viewtron, before closing it down in 1986. The vagueness of
such language was a thin mask for the questions, doubts, and confusion prevailing in the news business.[20]

The Tribune Company's vice president for technology, asked why
print media companies were rushing into electronic ventures, replied
sardonically, "Because everybody else is. . . . Everybody can't be
wrong, can they?" In 1995 Times Mirror budgeted almost $15 mil-
lion for new media initiatives in its magazine group, led by *Field and
Stream* and *Popular Science*. One of their former executives com-
mented, "They are trying to renew aging, dying publications by
throwing money at new media rather than saying, 'Which business
should we be in?' "[21]

THE TIMING OF the multiple, cumulative, and convergent crises in
the news business had been cruel, throwing orderly managerial cal-
culations into turmoil. For most of the 1980s, coterminous with
Reagan's "morning in America," industry leaders had ridden high,
still enjoying the richly profitable fruits of the computer revolution
and able to avert their eyes from indications of trouble ahead with
audiences and advertisers.

The escalation of those troubles coincided with recession as the 1990s began. That intensified confusion about which aspects of erosion of circulation, advertising, and profit were merely cyclical and which were systemic. The confusion, given hard times and pessimism about the future, in turn impaired the battered industry's ability to deal with the troublesome behavior of its two significant others. In declaring a dismissive independence, one of them — advertising — had at least been candid about it. The other — the audience — was fickle, cryptic, and teasing, impossible to please.

Give folks straight news and they say they want good news and by the way stop being biased. Give them good news and somebody calls it infotainment, and nobody likes it any better than straight news anyway. Give them a breakneck investigative exposé and nobody can get enough and then somebody calls it a feeding frenzy and suddenly everybody hates "the media" . . .

That was the familiar syndrome. But how to put a handle on it all, understand it, contain it? No one had ventured much further into an overarching analysis than Jimmy Carter and his advisers in 1979 with their aborted diagnosis of a national "malaise." Stumbling around with nostrums and jargon like "customer obsession," the news business was in fact struggling with the nature of modern existence. To what outer boundaries of the contemporary environment could it ask people (whose parents and grandparents had followed the maps of armed engagement in Europe, the Pacific, and Korea) to extend their time and interest?

Instantaneous national and foreign news — "the CNN effect" — along with the collapse of the Soviet Union and end of the Cold War, blurred people's sense of distance and frame. Twenty years ago, the processing of news from the former Yugoslavia would have turned on the question of Soviet interests, as against ours. No longer; at various points in the 1990s our leaders referred to the crisis there as "a hiccup" (George Bush) and "a shooting gallery" (Bill Clinton).[22]

What was journalism's role in the interpretation of a hiccup? Especially if so much of the news of the day came across in the CNN format: as raw film, often shocking but out of context; as a twenty-four-hour mechanized buzz that seemed to make the day's newspaper irrelevant hours before it was delivered; as governmental leaders doing business in real time through the television medium (was that news, or theater; real, or make-believe?).[23]

Meanwhile, the marketing revolution meant that principles of geography and mission underlying the very concept of big metropolitan newspapers were at growing cross-purposes with their economics. "Television is now most people's primary source of national and international breaking news," noted an uncommonly thoughtful corporate planner, James Lessersohn of the New York Times Company, putting the dilemma this way: "Newspapers' core strength is still the local franchise. But when you look at the advertising side of the equation, you have this problem: You now have the niche magazine model of community of interest cutting across geographic boundaries, [as against] the newspaper model of community in terms of geography. Advertisers, who want maximum efficiency, too often prefer the magazine model."[24]

The point is this: demographic target marketing, backed by database compilation and management, is the essence of the new advertising, and of the new *niched* media formats — typically magazines. Newspapers' editorial and business raison d'etre is the opposite: it continues to assume a broad *general* interest, within geographically defined boundaries.

Newspapers can, and do, target pieces of the paper to those niched pieces of the market in order to serve advertisers. The trouble is that here, as in their rush to soften their news mission, the more they make such a premise the governing one, the more they contort themselves, and distort what they were born to do.

The more they do so, furthermore, the more they undermine the dual propositions that have for so long linked the fate of the American press to the fate of the nation: First, the proposition that a functioning democracy depends on linkages of interest rather than separation and segmented targeting of them. Second, the proposition that the press, in search of mass audiences, is instrumental to those linkages.

NINE

Trying Something

DESPERATE TO REVERSE the losses, striving for coherence, at odds with time and space, the major news organizations
searched for the magic bullet that would help them recover circulation and advertising revenue. Some executives were sweeping in
their claims, some more odd-lot. Most formulations suggested the
triumph of gimmickry and promotion over substance and depth.
Most of them smacked of the tenuous, Micawber-like hope that if
the right heads just got together, if the right formula could just be
devised, happy results would ensue. As Jim Batten — the most reflective of the lot — had put it, we have to try *something*.

Knight-Ridder's "Project 25/43" premiered in Florida at the
chain's *Boca Raton News* in 1990, designed and heavily promoted to
attract the younger, television-oriented market. The Boca project
created a buzz in the trade press (what *were* the shrewd Knight-
Ridder chain managers up to?), along with some ridicule for what
The Columbia Journalism Review called the paper's "menu of news
McNuggets and its *Miami Vice*–pastel decor, including the pink
flamingo on the masthead." Taking its lead from focus group findings, the Boca project amounted to little more than "packaging" of
news content based on the *USA Today* model. For a while, Jim Batten
called the *Boca Raton News* his "weapons lab" for Knight-Ridder in
enticing busy baby boomers into daily readership of newspapers. But
the results were indifferent and the talk faded; Knight-Ridder papers
would pursue their obsession with customers individually. (In 1997

Knight-Ridder quietly unloaded the *Boca Raton News* to a lesser chain.)[1]

Gannett unveiled its "News 2000" program the following year, featuring a pyramid of ten topics to be focused on by the chain's eighty-one papers. "Community interest" formed the base of the pyramid; surveys, focus groups, and readership studies to determine that interest with specificity were the order of the day. Corporate headquarters monitored individual papers' and their executives' performance.[2]

The Orange County Register assigned a reporter to cover shopping malls full time and ran seasonal boxes listing the shopping hours for local malls on the front page of the paper. Knight-Ridder's *Miami Herald,* reeling from job cuts and commands to increase profit margins over previous years, announced in 1995 that based on in-depth reader surveys it would focus henceforth on nine topics: local government, education, sports, environment, consumer news, Florida news, health and medicine, Latin America, and crime. Missing from the list were world affairs, national politics, and economics. The editor told his staff that he hadn't read a story about Bosnia in two years, adding, "A reader — even a high-minded, liberal-thinking one with a world view — wants to know, 'What does this mean to ME?' "[3]

The American Society of Newspaper Editors issued a report called "Keys to Our Survival" based on research by another of the industry's favorite researchers, Kris McGrath of the opinion-polling firm MORI, that focused on saving "at-risk readers" and securing "potential" ones. Estimating that these categories together constituted 26 percent of the public, the report was a model of how the news business translates the shallowest, most debatable of findings into the latest in lockstep doctrine. The typical "at-risk" reader, in the report's shorthand, "wants news presented quickly, easy and fun," "feels harried and unable to control events," and "retreats to protected, provincial world." The typical "potential" one is "seriously interested in events, hard news" but is distracted by "major life changes" and "pressed for time." The report featured "targeted prototypes" for new sections. One for "at-risk readers" prepared at *The*

Orange County Register carried a description by the paper's then editor, Chris Anderson, that spoke volumes about the reactive mindset of many top news executives: "In line with MORI findings, we decided to make the section's personality more 'tabloid' than the current style. Headlines are bigger, louder. Stories are shorter. (At-risk readers want simplicity, more emotion in news presentation.)"[4]

News executives struggled to articulate a vision of a reinvented "personal connection" with their readers. "We are trying to get out of the business of being the mediator between our readers and the news and into the business of listening over the back fence while people talk," said one of them, Jerry Ceppos, executive editor of Knight-Ridder's *San Jose Mercury News*.[5]

MEETING IN SOLEMNITY at the annual convention of the American Society of Newspaper Editors and similar conclaves, top news executives took racial and ethnic tensions seriously. They fastened with enthusiasm on the vaguely defined model of multicultural diversity as a means to recover lost ground: it had the ring of a metropolitan area's universe of neighborhoods. Newsrooms themselves were white and male preserves to absurd extents in modern times. The language of "multiculturalism" as a way of talking (or not talking) about society and its problems seemed to blend with a way of grappling with those of the news business and its workforce.

Were black, Hispanic, and Asian populaces indifferent to the mainstream press? Were women and gays offended by its conscious or unconscious sexism? Was the press missing an opportunity to build its reach into communities that considered themselves marginalized? News organizations held retreats to strategize new approaches to community coverage, to engage in racial and gender sensitivity training, to devise sensitive language usage guides for their copy desks.

But the politics of the street came into the newsroom along with high-minded exhortations. Suddenly newsrooms had de facto caucuses organized by gender, race, and ethnicity. Suddenly coverage of controversial stories had to be negotiated within the newsroom as well as outside, and tensions over them revealed the extent to which co-workers had trouble even speaking to one another.

When urban racial tensions raged out of control, as they did over and over again in Los Angeles, New York, and elsewhere in the 1990s, it became clear that, internally, the press had come to reflect a new American dilemma. Diplomatic language and arrangements permit hostile nations to coexist and even do business. In the racially troubled United States, the press along with other mainstream institutions negotiated frantically to keep the peace within as a requirement of functioning organizationally in relation to their outside constituencies. Like universities, they put domestic equivalents of diplomatic accommodation into use, along with hiring quotas: "diversity committees" to police their own performance as employers, their own uses of language, alleged slips into "racial stereotyping." Was it harder for reporters and editors to convey to readers and viewers such background facts as that an act of violence occurred in a "high-crime neighborhood" if that phrase was judged a racially insensitive usage? Such were the prices required to keep racial tension and mistrust under control, inside newsrooms as in society.[6]

And yet within newsrooms and outside them divisions were so profound, charges of bad faith and double standards so pervasive, that the concept of "white justice" and a separate black version (it was suggested in the wake of the O. J. Simpson case) simply had to be accepted, and covered by the press as such.[7]

TELEVISION EXECUTIVES HIRED "news doctors" to make over their nightly news broadcasts, to guide them into "happy talk" atmospherics and news formulas devised and tested in pilot markets. These were the notorious "if it bleeds, it leads" tabloid formats, packaged with "news lite" features, consumer items, and a good deal of weather. The news doctors prescribed age, ethnic, and gender specifications for anchor team lineups to assure maximum penetration of target demographic groups.[8]

The networks "have never been easily embarrassed when it comes to money," Walter Goodman remarked; nevertheless the public sometimes forced them back from shamelessness. One of the networks' innovations, faked "reenactment" of events to make the broadcast more visually dramatic, provoked a bad reaction from viewers as well as critics, and was dropped. In Chicago in 1997, the NBC-owned television station's decision to drive its evening news broadcasts downmarket by recruiting "trash TV" talk-show host Jerry Springer to do nightly commentaries backfired. The station's respected news co-anchor resigned in protest, viewers expressed their disgust with the measures being taken to please them, and the station folded its strategy and removed its chief.[9]

But the overall trend was relentlessly a function of television's essence as an entertainment medium, often accelerated by the more recent media mergers that put news organizations in thrall to commercial entertainment giants and the profit imperative. The new industry economics meant filling airtime with low-budget "documentaries" reprocessed from video libraries. "Synergy" meant that NBC news programs promoted NBC entertainment phenomena like the farewell of its prime-time show *Seinfeld*. ABC News promoted ABC's prime-time *Ellen,* as well as the latest from parent company Disney's entertainment production line and even the doings of Disney chairman Michael Eisner.[10]

A sign of the times was ABC News executives' spiking of an investigative piece on Disney theme parks "for a whole variety of reasons," as an ABC spokeswoman put it with sweet guilelessness, "one of which is that whatever [ABC News might] come up with [in reporting on Disney], positive or negative, will seem suspect." Another was the bargain NBC News made in 1998 with Geraldo Rivera. When Rupert Murdoch's Fox News Channel sought to lure the maestro of self-promotional tabloid television from CNBC, NBC News countered by settling a six-year, $30 million contract on him. Rivera leaped from the uninhibited world of cable to his own program in a prime-time NBC News slot, complete with live support from NBC News correspondents. "In this partnership," *The New York Times* reported, "Mr. Rivera gives NBC news ratings; NBC News gives him instant respectability."[11]

NEWSPAPERS TRIED AUDIOTEXT services (now you could dial up racing results and soap opera plot summaries). They refined their schemes for collaborations with advertisers based on the sharing of computerized database research and information about readers and consumers. They maneuvered to thwart the designs of telephone and software companies to steal their classified advertising franchise. And newspapers imagined the ultimate deus ex machina, somewhat in the manner of Jules Verne. This was an interactive, electronic, "tailored" newspaper of the future, adaptable to individual tastes and interests, centerpiece of all-purpose digital access to news, information, and service. Going further, they saw themselves evolving into fully integrated "information content providers," building (as a Tribune Company executive put it) "the media network of the 21st century": supple, synergistic, and flexible communications systems defying old-order categories like "print," "broadcast," and "computer." Unclear was the question whether great numbers of tomorrow's consumers of news and information would prefer, in the long run, to narrowcast and niche themselves, making the choices that the tailored newspaper machinery assumes, or to have them made for them more, or less, as the press makes them today.[12]

NONE OF THESE initiatives probed in depth the trajectory of the nation's fortunes, the nature of modern American life, the troubles plaguing the American psyche. Only by delving into such topics could the news business have developed an inner-directed (as distinct from marketing-driven) base of intelligence about the meaning and nature of news in a time of loss, and of the public's internalized relation to it, beyond what pollsters can glean at the surface. Instead, the news business continued on with its litany of truisms: people are busy, distracted, and tired of "bad news" . . . kids aren't developing the newspaper habit . . . the TV generation has limited attention span and itchy remote control fingers . . . the public is segmented according to lifestyle . . . a multicultural society requires recognition of separate, individualized interests.[13]

Furthermore, none of these initiatives faced squarely up to the multimillion-dollar question challenging news industry leaders: Can the press, under modern conditions, retain both its standards and its economics? Can newspapers in particular remain viable vehicles of mass communication? One of the hard answers — the audience for serious journalism is shrinking to niche-market dimensions — was inadmissible to most publishers and editors alike. Another —

maintenance of mass numbers means making journalism more "popular" — merely made trouble in the newsroom.

In the recession years of the '90s, retrenching in order to maintain corporate profit margins with a vengeance, news industry executives tended to state the case to disgruntled editors and reporters this way: "We're a business, and in order to survive as a vehicle for news and information according to high standards (translation: keep you self-righteous journalists employed), we have to adjust to market realities." Persuasive enough as a rationale, this formulation masked the fact that in place of the traditional balancing act by which the press maintained itself as a public trust as well as a business, a priority had been established: Wall Street was a more important constituency than those for whom the news was reported and edited.

This became plain enough in 1994, as the recession began to ease. Just then the newsprint industry — a kind of rogue force that follows its own short-term, idiosyncratic cycles of supply and demand — slammed newspapers and magazines with a series of hefty price increases. In fact, newspapers had benefited from a slump in newsprint prices during the recession, so their cries of pain in the mid-1990s were really a complaint about timing, in the context of the escalating pressure from Wall Street to meet profit margin goals at all costs. But rather than treating the newsprint price flurry as the one, sure, short-term adjustment that it was in the pounding hurricane of adversity besetting the business, publishers used it instead to justify further deep cuts into news and editorial budgets, space, and workforces.[14]

WITH THE IMPROVEMENT in economic conditions in the late '90s, and with cost cutting in place (often at the expense of newsroom strength), news business executives took up the do-more-with-less script and demanded growth. Few promised it as rashly as Mark Willes of Times Mirror, who in 1997 committed *The Los Angeles Times* to a circulation increase of 500,000, 50 percent more than the newspaper's daily circulation of a million. The *Times* was already carrying a monumental and expensive burden of replacing lost home delivery subscribers with new ones, or "churn." (In 1997 Willes said the *Times*'s churn rate was an astounding 85 percent a year, or 19 percentage points above the industry averages; in 1998 he said it was more than 90 percent.)[15]

In so doing the corporate chiefs assumed, as industry economics and culture have long dictated, the fundamental goal of retaining, even expanding, mass medium status. They bounced back to the newsroom the riddle whether determined retention of that status, or something like it, dictates the gradual abandonment of journalism according to the higher standards and practices aspired to for more than a century.

An exception to this pattern of superficial analysis, quick fix, and dogma had come in 1991 from an unexpected source: the publishers themselves, organized then as the American Newspapers Publishers Association. A task force of the association staffed by bright young planners and managers produced a "competitive analysis" report taking account of "the role of technology in the competitive media environment," and posing four optional courses that any newspaper "can use to select a strategy that's right for its size, priorities, competitive position and goals."

Daringly, the report posed "the class appeal" as its second strategy, as against "the mass appeal," its first. Where the mass strategy would "follow the market" and "keep [market] share," driving newspaper content downmarket as needed ("more Madonna than Mozart"), "the class appeal" would do the opposite. It would accept the proposition that "the mass market is dead" and operate "as the targeted business it has already become," making up lost revenue in aggressive pricing to a committed audience willing to pay for a quality product, and to advertisers who want those readers.

The report offered two more options. One, "the individual appeal," would add print products tailored to readers' special interests. The other, "the direct appeal," would layer a local direct marketing enterprise over the daily paper, following steps some papers had already taken in that direction.

Intriguingly, the task force's projections for its options showed that while all four scenarios wound up with more or less the same bottom line over a decade, "the class appeal" would bring back the greatest profit, at least for a while.[16]

The arguments developed in these pages might logically lead to the question, why not — assuming an improvement on the impolitic "class appeal" phrasing — pursue that course, let the numbers fall to their own level, and cease the effort to drive newspapers into softer (or more tabloid), fuzzier (or more sensational), lowest-common-denominator (or more segmented) distortions of themselves in pursuit of an indifferent, elusive mass audience? Why not put out newspapers for people who care? Why not accept the reality that the quality press can retain mass market status only by measures that destroy its inherent value?

In fact, *The New York Times* and *The Wall Street Journal,* with their prestige, national circulation, and locks on certain forms of advertising, can speak in such terms and even practice them. But their situation is distinctive.

The New York Times reaches only 10 percent of the households in its metropolitan market daily and only 14 percent on Sundays; but its national circulation has become a stronger and stronger asset for it, and by many measures it is now a national paper, not a metropolitan one.

The situation outside New York takes several forms. *The Los Angeles Times* reaches 22 percent daily and 29 percent Sunday; the *Chicago Tribune* 20 percent daily and 32 percent Sunday. With such low penetration of their metropolitan markets, those papers are de facto demographically targeted; they are de facto out of the mass market and engaged in the "class appeal." It follows that they stand to make their money, like target-audience magazines, from strong, demographically organized circulation and advertising bases willing to pay high prices.[17]

But in other markets, quality newspapers manage to achieve considerably higher penetration rates. *The Washington Post,* for example, heavy on "metro," Maryland, and Virginia coverage, prides itself on its 47 percent daily penetration of the Washington-area market and 62 percent penetration on Sunday. Were a paper like *The Washington Post* to attempt to follow the "class appeal" and make up circulation and advertising losses with high pricing, it would tie itself in knots trying to turn into a magazine, distorting the organizing principle of the metropolitan newspaper business franchise: its broad circulation base. By contrast, Peter Kann, publisher of *The Wall Street Journal,* states candidly that his newspaper, publishing five days a week and attracting "an audience of unmatched intelligence, influence and affluence," is not a general interest publication at all and, as such, "competes much more directly with magazines than with any newspaper for high quality advertising."[18]

SO AS A MATTER of identity as well as a business proposition, most newspapers are stuck with the fact that geography is destiny: they exist to inform a broad community. And there is another issue, that of basic function and identity. And here we turn back to the opening pages of this book.

The news business in America was for so many decades a mass market enterprise because — discounting interludes of escapism, as in the 1920s — the United States was a vibrant democratic republic. Millions and millions of its citizens engaged with the politics and news of the day, from hometowns to the national and international arenas. They enjoyed taking their news in tandem with their consideration of what personal, family, or household needs to meet, what entertainment or leisure choices to make. Thus the self-image of many people in the business could be that they were, if not actually doing well by doing good, at least engaged in a line of work that was integral to the way democracy works. They were in the business of assuring an informed public, with advertising — dynamic gear of an expanding consumer economy — paying the freight.

Jim Squires, late of the *Chicago Tribune,* notes sardonically that such a formulation is also "the legal basis on which the printed press has always stood before legislatures and courts wrapped in the flag of the First Amendment," for nowhere do First Amendment protections "define 'the people' as the predominantly white upper 35 percent of the population between 25 and 50 years of age who make $50,000 a year."[19]

The erosion of the idea that everybody out there cares, or at least has a stake in the stuff of news, therefore carries weight for people in the news business that goes far beyond any range of task force options. It goes to the heart of the long-lived linkage between press culture and national culture, a linkage that says that deep down, if faith with traditions of professionalism are kept, journalism is public service for the many.

That linkage, once a talisman for journalists and their bosses, has been breaking down, for the variety of reasons examined in these pages. *It is part of a contemporary democratic crisis.* But it has so far proved impossible for news business executives to deal with that breakdown in ways that move beyond the confines of industry shoptalk, to acknowledge it as more than a threat to be responded to with better graphics, "repackaging," editing by focus group, and marketing.

Indeed, the industry's most frequent response to its breakdown has been its ritual self-flagellation for "elitism": if only we can get closer to what people think, say, like, hope, fear, we can solve our problems. Taken out the window as it has been, this reflex translates as: if only we could figure out how to stop being opinion leaders, and succeed as opinion followers, we could restore our numbers. But beyond the homilies, the Sphinx at Thebes could not have posed a more forbidding riddle than the one the press was struggling to identify, let alone answer: how can you get closer to what people think if they (together with their putative leaders) don't know what they think; when their loss and confusion cries out for a leadership that fails to materialize?

INTO THE UTTER vacuum in visionary thinking about the press and its problems in the mid-1990s strode the brash Mark Willes. No one else in the news business was shaking it up at that juncture, so let us pause on Willes for a moment.

In 1997, two years into his tenure as CEO of the struggling, once almighty Times Mirror Corporation, Willes had not only laid off thousands of the company's employees, closed down *New York Newsday,* killed nine zoned editions of *The Los Angeles Times,* axed the corporation's computer-age research and development think tank, unloaded several other unprofitable Times Mirror properties, including its People and the Press survey research operation, and displaced the respected publisher of the company's flagship, *The Los Angeles Times,* and added that job to his own. He had also driven the price of Times Mirror stock up to nearly three times what it had been when he arrived in 1995 and enabled his partners in his game plan, the corporation's board, to increase its annual divided.[20]

The noise Willes made in his "cereal killer" mode guaranteed a close watch on him by others in the business. A year after he had taken over, a *The New York Times* headline asked, "At Times Mirror, What's the Plan?" — beyond "shock treatment" retrenchment. That season, Willes's response was that growth "will come from ideas developed by Times Mirror's operating groups. [Willes said his] job 'is to try very hard to create an environment, and an expectation, so that we will grow.' Almost daily, Mr. Willes urges his staff to present ideas for new ventures." But, the reporter deadpanned, "so far, . . . no Times Mirror editor can name a special project that is going ahead."[21]

Fifteen months later, operating simultaneously as field officer and supreme commander, CEO Willes was ready with his own plan. As publisher of *The Los Angeles Times,* he revealed his amazing 50 percent circulation growth target for the paper; next, he marked for demolition the legendary "wall" between the industry's news-editorial and business sides, also known as the division between church (news) and state (business).

Each section of the *Times* would have its own business manager with responsibility for "maximizing readership and the financial performance," reporting to a new, overall general manager for news (previously the paper's senior vice president for consumer marketing). Each section would develop a strategic plan for growth: "readership objectives and revenue objectives," as Willes put it. Most sections would have to justify their existence in profit and loss terms. Special provision would be made for the main news section, but it too would "need to be measured" in readership improvement. Section editors and the new business managers would be expected to "partner" on ideas for growth, including new and revamped sections.

Said Willes of the wall-no-more, "I don't think there is a fundamental problem saying that ideas ought to be coming from the business side and the editorial side. . . . Having said that, I would be surprised and disappointed if most of the ideas didn't come from the business side." In other words, the elements of the paper, like the paper as a whole, are businesses; at *The Los Angeles Times* as in

most of the industry, these businesses are under the direction of editors who institutionally and culturally are stricken with no-growth
paralysis; the wall has meant that the business side of the operation
is forbidden to interfere; so, in other words, in sending the business
side over the wall, I expect it to exorcise paralysis.[22]

Willes, a devout Mormon, was a familiar type in American life:
the businessman as Boy Scout and zealot, missionary reformer and
corporate achiever, as if Sinclair Lewis had crossed George Bab-
bitt with Elmer Gantry in an old-fashioned cocktail, adding a nice
squirt of Wendell Willkie for good measure. Willkie tried to translate
his free-thinking business approach to politics, his passion making
up for his amateurishness — and gave FDR, the champ, the closest of
his four presidential races. Willes presumed that the systems he'd
mastered — financial management and marketing — were translata-
ble to the stricken news business.

Other publishers had been experimenting with elements of the
plan Willes concocted for news- and business-side collaboration,
without throwing down the gauntlet and laying personal claim to a
new industry paradigm. But Willes's patience for the niceties of a
business so profoundly ill, one he'd been recruited into precisely
because of its sickness, was about zero. Like the driven makers of the
modern news business of generations past — Hearst, McCormick,
Patterson, Graham, Luce, Paley — Willes wanted to get his hands
dirty on the nuts and bolts of the business and personally wrestle its
ephemeral elements to the ground, as if will would prevail where
lesser men had failed. In an industry led by the battle-weary officers of
the last war, he was, whatever else, a fascinating work-in-progress.[23]

SHELBY COFFEY, AN accomplished journalist and editor of *The Los
Angeles Times* for eight years and of Times Mirror's *Dallas Times
Herald* before that, resigned on the occasion of Willes's unfurling of
his down-with-the-wall plan. Former editors of major newspapers,
including Ben Bradlee of *The Washington Post,* Max Frankel of *The
New York Times,* and me, were interviewed for comment and were
critical of Willes. Willes was unimpressed and took his message to
forum after forum, attacking his press critics for prejudging his mo-
tives and actions. I, for example, was quoted in *The New York Times*

in the fall of 1997 saying that his plan was "part of this desperate search for formulas to make the numbers come out right," and that "the point about journalistic rules and standards and the walls that have long existed between the business and news people is that they are there for the long run. When you take away the barriers you create scenarios where very ambitious people can play around."

Ingenuously or disingenuously, Willes took comments like mine about news business culture in general personally. "What these people are saying is our own editors don't have the standards or backbone to stand up to the pressures" of advertisers and other interested outsiders, Willes told the reporter who quoted me. "What they're really doing is impugning the strength and integrity of our own editors."[24]

In one of his missionary appearances Willes wept as he described the kind of story he wanted to see in his papers — he was increasingly functioning as editor of *The Los Angeles Times* in all but name, as well as its publisher. (His case in point was about Los Angeles children caught in drug-trade gunfire.) He announced a scheme for quantifiable increases in the number of women and minorities quoted in *The Los Angeles Times* and other Times Mirror papers to reflect "the diversity of the community that we're both reporting on and want to be read by." Incentive pay would be awarded to editors on the basis of achievement of that goal. In an aside he called for "more emotional, more personal, less analytical" stories in *The Los Angeles Times* in order to attract more women. Then he apologized to an angry staff for "comments that seemed to stereotype women in an exceptionally unfortunate way."[25]

As in apologizing to the offended women at *The Los Angeles Times,* Willes understood that appearances counted, and he dutifully mouthed the traditional homilies about the integrity of news and editorial operations. "For any successful business, the product has to be perceived as special by the buyer or user," he told an interviewer. In the case of newspapers, he added, special status "has everything to do now with not just readability but with this important element of trust." But he showed no interest in the fact that the church-state wall was the traditional symbol of that trust, the internal institutional element that had set the press apart as a business.

The privileges guaranteed by the First Amendment were the external element. But inside, the wall had been the place where publishers' money had for about a century met their mouths, signaling that public trust was about unimpaired credibility on the news side, that the news and editorial content of a newspaper was more than just another "product."[26]

For Willes, history (as a corporate pioneer of an earlier era had put it) was "bunk": the profound roots of the news industry's troubles in political, social, and cultural disintegration in the United States held no interest for him. (If he'd had such interest, he would have held on to the Times Mirror Center for the People and the Press, the one survey outfit that focuses intensively on press audience issues in depth, and hardly a major capital drain on the corporation.)

No. The press was a business. Growth was essential. The tired careerists he'd succeeded and displaced simply didn't understand the "branding" potential of newspapers. A comprehensive product like a newspaper existed to be segmented; the segments were vehicles for target marketing of brands, to audiences, by interest — *Los Angeles Times* sports, *Los Angeles Times* personal finance, and so forth. Like a good mass market packaged-goods man, Willes hurled millions of dollars into a brand-marketing campaign and cut the newsstand price of *The Los Angeles Times*: he would show growth![27]

But with his vow to raise the paper's circulation by 50 percent, Willes tied himself to the tracks. No news executive in the country was watched more closely by Wall Street. If he succeeded, he'd be hailed as an industry genius. If he didn't, or if he achieved growth only at outlandish cost, Wall Street and his own corporate masters would be harsh judges. As if to anticipate them, with mid-1999 returns from his labors disappointing, Willes handed off the publishership of *The Los Angeles Times* to a protégé, having dispatched Times Mirror's annual report with the statement that failure of his newspaper growth strategies "would mean dismantling the company and returning capital to the shareholders" so they "could make their individual diversification decisions."[28] Either way, like his less bumptious news business colleagues, Willes had attacked a piece of the problem and missed the whole.

PART 4

Alternatives

TEN

Hamilton and Jefferson

ONE RESPONSE TO the plight of the news business was grounded in more intellectual and professional integrity than the others, and it tried to make the leap between the journalistic and political cultures. Moreover, its prophets neither promised nor expected "quick-fix" effects. Rather, they called for a reinvention of "public life" and of the press role in it as intermediary between government and the public.

This was the "civic journalism" movement of the early 1990s, also known as public journalism. It too was flawed, not for want of dedicated effort but because it bit off only half of the fundamental issue.

Civic journalism's most effective original impulse came from Jim Batten of Knight-Ridder. With a good reportorial eye, Batten noted the falling numbers for voting turnout and for newspaper readership in recent years, and he linked them.[1]

Batten made another connection as well. As chief executive officer of one of the most acquisitive newspaper chains in the country he observed that the disappearance of locally based families as proprietors of newspapers, and their replacement by deputies from the corporate offices of chains like his, were working against communities' sense that the local newspaper was theirs. He wondered what might be done by news organizations, making the most of their local franchises, to build up rather than erode the public's sense of connection to the life of the community, to news, to civic involvement.

Other ideas shaped the civic journalism initiative, especially those of reporter and columnist David Broder of *The Washington Post,* editor Davis ("Buzz") Merritt of Knight-Ridder's *Wichita Eagle,* and communications scholar Jay Rosen of New York University. Drawing on scholarly analyses of the decline of modern American public life, Rosen especially among the civic journalism advocates critiqued the mainstream press for taking skepticism about contemporary politics to excess. In "jeering" at politicians' contrived techniques of manipulative ads, media events, and spin "even as they tried to cover them, [journalists] joined in a culture of cynicism," wrote Rosen.[2]

But the movement would not have gone far without Batten's pragmatic interest in statistical data indicating real-world problems affecting the newspaper industry, observed in his capacity as an industry manager and leader. The nature of Batten's interest steadied the movement at the start, and his premature death in 1995 robbed it of an anchor later on.

The movement organized around the idea of civic journalism took form in a set of initiatives directed by Knight-Ridder and other news organizations, often with funding from foundations that responded directly to Batten's ideas and advocacy. The initiatives featured concerted, out-of-the-ordinary inquiry into what issues were on the public mind, and in-depth coverage of them in and out of election season with an emphasis on interactivity between news organization and citizens. Newspapers, sometimes in partnership with local television or radio stations, devoted pages and pages to these projects, assigned squadrons of reporters, editors, and graphic designers to them, ran them as heavily promoted specials or series, sometimes kicking them off with front-page statements from the editor or publisher. By these means, newspapers signaled that their civic journalism projects were a major break in routine.

The idea was two-step. First, "hear" readers on the specifics of such issues as education, taxes, urban development and regional planning, crime, race relations. Next, get political candidates and officials to respond to such concerns in a spirit of genuine exchange, forcing them off reliance on their staged, manipulative media campaigns.

These projects went beyond the usual rote focus group and survey technique. In some of the initiatives, local newspapers sponsored "town meetings" with elected officials and published excerpts from the proceedings in the pages of the newspaper. A governing idea was to make the news organization less the distant, detached bearer of news, and more the middleman and catalyst for a renewed vox populi in the public affairs of the community.

Conscious of the turnoff factor—the extent to which nonvoters and those disillusioned with the press believed their participation in public affairs made no difference—the civic journalism projects were heavy on service information and listings showing readers how to get involved with community or advocacy organizations. To their credit, industry figures at the center of the initiative, like Buzz Merritt of the *Wichita Eagle*, sought no early bang-for-the-buck payoff in circulation increases or other obvious indicators. They understood that, as erosion in newspapers' positions had been gradual, so would any recovery.

BY MANY MEASURES, the civic journalism movement caught the breakdown of connection between the press and the political life of the country. A number of thoughtful editors and publishers as well as press critics, scholars, and civic leaders admired its thrust. "Today's journalists can choose," wrote James Fallows in a sympathetic account of the movement: "Do they want merely to entertain the public or to engage it? . . . if journalists should choose to engage the public, they will begin a long series of experiments and decisions to see how journalism might better serve its fundamental purpose, that of making democratic self-government possible. They could start with the example set by public journalism and work on the obvious problems and limits of that model."[3]

The problems and limitations to which Fallows referred were several. Civic journalism prompted a bad reaction among some influential editors and reporters, especially on major papers like *The New York Times* and *The Washington Post*. They detected in the new gospel a pull away from hard-hitting, big-time journalism, and toward the endless siren songs from circulation and marketing departments to become more lovable in the eyes of critical and alienated audiences. (Indeed, at Knight-Ridder the linkage between the new corporate "customer obsession" mantra and civic journalism was fairly explicit.) They also saw in it a distortion of role, pushing newspapers too close to a posture of editorializing in their news pages, an echo of the bad old days when barons of the press frankly used their papers as extensions of their own political agendas.[4]

A few saw in civic journalism the stuff of artifice, formula, and distraction from the business of news. The inevitable translation of "the movement" into formula was evident at what a Knight-Ridder editor in the mid-1990s described to me as a command performance by him and his counterparts at the chain's other papers at a meeting to review their respective civic journalism projects for the coming quarters — entries on a management-by-objectives grid.

The civic journalism idea worked best for newspapers in mid-sized, relatively cohesive cities. On the Knight-Ridder chain's map, those were places like Wichita, Kansas, and Charlotte, North Carolina. They were not Knight-Ridder cities like Philadelphia, Detroit, and Miami, where racial, ethnic, and class divisions of massive proportions ran too deep for civic togetherness or the town meeting approach to be realistic measures or goals.

Gene Roberts, who as executive editor of *The Philadelphia Inquirer* resisted pressure from Jim Batten and his corporate colleagues at Knight-Ridder to cut budgets for news operations, put it this way: "It's much cheaper for publishers to run civic journalism series in the paper, and hold a lot of meetings, than to invest in space and staff and budget for news."[5]

To Roberts, former executive editor Max Frankel of *The New York Times,* executive editor Len Downie of *The Washington Post,* and others who agreed with them, "civic journalism" was a softened-down, gimmicked-up version of the kind of hard-driving engagement with issues that bigger, stronger, more enterprising papers like theirs practiced as a matter of course, year in and out.

THE LINES OF argument about civic journalism hardened. Increasingly the movement saw its mission as intramural, within the profession. Fallows compared its leaders to the "military reform" movement that had forced the American military establishment to learn the lessons of its failures in Vietnam. Indeed, the civic journalism advocates, including Fallows, grew angry in their indictment of old-style journalism for its persistence in tearing down politicians and deepening the public's disgust with politics and news.

Condemning reporters, editorialists, and headline writers at *The New York Times* and *The Washington Post* for piling onto Bill Clinton's fumbling in his first weeks and months in office, Jay Rosen wrote, "The moral universe of the Washington press virtually begins and ends" with a "low realism" that values "above all . . . a quality we can label savviness — an insider's knowledge of how the game is played."[6]

Fallows wrote that both the Bush and Clinton administrations "have been sneered at and treated as if everything they did was a ruse, and this is because of a change in the press's attitude in the last twenty years. The working assumption for most reporters is that most politicians and handlers will mislead them most of the time. The coverage we see is a natural result — which aggravates today's prevailing despair and cynicism about public life."[7]

Here lay the biggest limitation for the civic journalism idea, more serious than the fact that as a movement to reform journalism it had succeeded in making enemies of the two most influential daily papers in the country, *The New York Times* and *The Washington Post*. In focusing on "a change in the press's attitude in the last twenty years" but neglecting the corresponding changes in the political sphere, the reformers contributed to a slippage of the debate into name-calling within the profession.

The reformers aimed away from the problematic environmental context in which a flawed and troubled journalistic culture was attempting to maintain a footing against an ever more corrupted, ever more manipulative, ever more dead-end, ever more cynical political profession. They demonstrated at best a limited historical or current appreciation of the *critical* function of journalism in a good society, or the squalid realities with which, in the actual politics of journalism, these unwashed reporters and editors have been contending in the age of image management. They invited comparison with the single-issue reformers of earlier times, the good-government Mugwumps of the late nineteenth century and the righteous Prohibitionists of the early twentieth. Indeed, civic journalism sought to indoctrinate cynical G.I. Joe reporters with civic values, to instill in them that they must be about "not only a critique of public institutions but an invigoration of public spaces," in Rosen's words.[8]

Working on the civic journalism model the press can achieve small, limited, localized victories against the backdrop of a national breakdown. But it remains at best a Jeffersonian approach to a Hamiltonian dilemma.[9]

WHAT'S MISSING FROM the civic journalism concept is recognition of the extent to which the press operates, particularly in Washington, in the political culture. The relationship between the press and the political culture is mutually obsessive; each is a variation on a love-hate pattern. Each works to seduce, manipulate, and distance itself from the other. Each seeks at once degrees of intimacy with the other and degrees of elusiveness.

But in Washington as elsewhere, the political culture tends to be the dominant one. That dominance is traditional, tracing back to the time of newspapers as party organs. The balance shifted for a while as the modern press came into its own in the 1960s and 1970s, riding high on its work in Vietnam and Watergate, and on the epic Supreme Court decisions that had the effect of supporting that work. But the time, after Watergate, of press preeminence happened to coincide with the decline of the old fabric of national power, exercised abroad and at home on the Roosevelt and Truman models. And it happened to coincide with the metamorphosis of the new politics into a money and media game, with the emphasis on manipulation. These happenstances of timing guaranteed that the balance of power between politics and press would become a slipping gear.

Indeed, the victories for the press over government news managers in Vietnam and Watergate worked as provocations to the military and the political profession to mobilize on the public relations front to assure no repetition of such debacles. When the dust settled, the relative pecking order of the political and press cultures was as it used to be — even as the transformation within the political and press cultures had been sweeping. For as the political profession assimilated the lessons of the 1960s and 1970s, as it married itself to television and other modern media formats, it developed fresh momentum and morale. As was evident in the Pentagon's airtight news management in the Persian Gulf War, and Clinton's war-footing press policy through the Lewinsky scandal, not a little of that momentum and morale was fueled by revenge against the press.

Today, the political profession has far outpaced the press's effort to keep up with its command of the modern arts of persuasion, its integrated mobilization of communications media and public relations. The political professionals have achieved a strategic mastery of computerized polling, television advertising, "media event," leaked and placed news story, preemptive command of the news cycle, manipulation of opponents' "negatives"; all the database management and marketing techniques that go into "issue management." Thus, the political profession has single-mindedly mobilized the elements of modern media to advance agenda, take hits, achieve goals, win. The press has not.

Is the press bigger, more ubiquitous, louder, more brazenly intrusive than ever? Yes. Is its power monstrous to individuals caught in the full blaze of its blinding lights and thundering machinery? Without question. Is its maneuverability on the ground a match for that of political news managers in full spin? No, not given the fickleness of public concern, especially not when economic times are bright. Press power today is huge, but raw and undisciplined, at times incoherent in operation. By contrast, political power today is a streamlined instrument of cutthroat marketing and virtual war.

What the press is left with is the catch-up mode. At the core of its strength is the very traditional ability to expose just how contrived the actual structure of political power is, based as it is today not on the force of effective governance or coalition party politics but on media-based techniques of opinion management.

Scholarly critics like Paul Weaver and Thomas Patterson have faulted the press for having moved — years before marketplace pressures started driving it toward "infotainment" — to covering politics more and more as a "game," in the process "strengthening the voters' mistrust of the candidates and reducing their sense of involvement." Writes Patterson, "When journalists encounter new information during an election, they tend to interpret it within a schematic framework according to which candidates compete for advantage.

The candidates play the game well or poorly. . . . Whereas the game was once viewed as the means, it is now the end, while policy problems, issues, and the like are mere tokens" in campaigns. The Patterson view holds that the "game" mind-set of the press cheats the citizenry out of fair consideration of politicians' ideas and policy proposals, out of discussion of issues.[10]

This view is not wrong, but it goes only so far. On a historical level, it fails to take into account that some of the modern press impulse to cast itself as such a chronic skeptic springs from its self-correction in the wake of the McCarthy era, when all agreed it had focused much too literally on what the senator said and much too little on the diabolical game he was playing. (A growing challenge for the twenty-first-century press, it might be agreed, is that given its force and the swift pace and complexities of modernity, it's under ever more pressure to function self-correctively as to what it covers and how.)

Patterson himself acknowledges that "game" coverage in the press evolved in pace with the decline of the old politics, featuring strong local and state organizations and brokered conventions, and the emergence of the new politics featuring media campaigning in sweepstake primary after primary across the country. Thus he perceives that the press and politicians are interactive. Yet like most press critics, his focus and emphasis are singularly on the press, not on the larger picture. What does not emerge in such an analysis is the intricate tango of political and press cultures — the dance of spin and exposure of it, the negative synergy of a game it takes two to play.[11]

A revealing piece of the action not visible to the public is the de rigueur ritual of the candidate's campaign-season call on the editors, political reporters, and editorial writers of the major news organizations. There, over lunch or coffee, with the publisher's presence and the candidate's entourage rendering the event a state visit, the candidate seeks to dazzle the journalists with word of his or her recruitment of top-ranked campaign consultants and pollsters from the mercenary ranks, of the campaign's consequent, unbeatably shrewd reading of the public mood, of its consequent, ingenious fund-raising and media strategies — in short, of her or his game plan.

There's time of course for the candidate to display an intimate ease with issues large and small. But that part of the exercise, too, is conducted as something of a game, partly for its tactical effect on journalism's backbenchers, the editorial writers who will help decide and shape the news organization's formal endorsement. (Since JFK the idea has been for the candidate to display not so much thoughtfulness or vision as computer-crisp command of detail and data, and thus competence and — key insider criterion for judging the modern politico — *good staffing*.)

At *The Boston Globe* we got not only the statewide candidates but all the national ones testing the waters in New Hampshire, or fresh from the kickoff presidential primary there. And so we got them at perhaps a peak moment of stars in their eyes as to their potential for the playing field. The heavyweights as to knowledge of government, years in politics, an intellect or at least a well-seasoned point of view, like Mario Cuomo and John Connally, managed the whole package of self-presentation ably as visitors on a closed circuit. Their entourages were extraneous baggage. But in the end, their strengths, and what modern politics had become, did not fit and they dropped out. The race went instead to the glib, the well managed, the well programmed, coiffed and cued for television, the George Bushes and the John F. Kerrys.

"These days, the tool kit of the successful challenger's campaign includes a simple message repeated endlessly, an elbows-out style, an agility with sound-bites, a ferocious pace and a faith in . . . television advertising," goes the wisdom of "political operatives," as reported in a press obituary for an "old politics" figure (1998 Connecticut Democratic gubernatorial candidate Barbara B. Kennelly). The fact is that elections today are organized ever more around money for nonstop negative television spots conceived and executed by the mercenaries. "Issues" are ever more the reductive content of those ads, fabricated by the mercenaries from polling and focus group indications of what's selling in a given season and what isn't. The candidate is ever more a pawn in the game rather than its master strategist.[12]

In fact, the political profession often has more to fear from advocacy groups armed with "wedge issue" agendas of their own than from the mainstream press. Thus, the reporting of a major story focuses on the question whether a weak administration in Washington is winning or being outgunned in the "issues management" struggle with an adversary interest group, as was the Clinton administration in its losing campaign for universal health care.

THE DOMINANCE OF political culture over press culture also means that journalism inclines, in its love-hate cycles, toward a parasitical and imitative relationship as well as an adversarial and critical one. Some years ago, Jim Fallows himself was one of the first to catch the emergence of the Washington reporter as TV know-it-all and trade association speaker for show-business fees, and to note the intellectual as well as professional conflicts of interest flowing from this harvest. But such ways of plying the journalistic trade are really a matter of adaptation to the political culture, itself adapting to entertainment and celebrity culture.

Political culture being dominant in relation to press culture, it rather than the press is the place to look for the deeper problem and the deeper fault. As to cynicism, what sin of the press was more corrosive to the democratic idea in recent history than, in the administration of the virtuous Jimmy Carter, the precedent-setting insertion of presidential campaign pollster Patrick Caddell into the top level of White House day-to-day policymaking? (Unless I've missed something in the literature, even Caddell didn't have the gall to claim that this was a measure designed to enhance responsible democratic government.) The centrality of image management by Mike Deaver and his team in the Reagan White House? The Bush campaign of 1988, effectively focusing the electorate in these times on the American flag, the pledge of allegiance, and the Willie Horton case? The insouciance with which Bill Clinton, a master of the universe of denial, dissembled about his past and turned on Dick Morris's polling dime?

Have the discrediting of government and the collapse of the old, multidimensional party system had devastating effects on American politics? The press is not in the business of developing such wide-angle perspectives. Most of its waking hours go to tracking the workings of the new system — Bill Clinton operating as he does, his challengers and would-be successors as they do, the contemporary political money game as it does. Civic journalism can't remedy so fundamental a structural deterioration.

ELEVEN

Therefore . . .

GIVEN THE ODDS against which journalists work of late, given the extent to which so many journalists themselves have accepted the various doctrines of the news business rialto — from "lighten up" to "relationship marketing" — it's astonishing that those who have followed their own professional standards and instincts have prevailed to the extent that they have.

Most news organizations today still attract reporters, writers, and editors of fine ability and high integrity. It's in the blood. In the newsrooms of many of them, the pursuit of news and interpretation, facts and background, as distinct from the devising of decoration, infotainment, and hype, are still what the work is about. And some of them publish and broadcast results as distinguished as they've ever been. A case in point is the reporting in the 1990s from the former Yugoslavia by brave young reporters for *The Christian Science Monitor,* CNN, *The New York Times, Newsday, The Philadelphia Inquirer, The Washington Post,* and several other outlets, which follows on the work of only slightly older counterparts in Central and South America and elsewhere in Eastern Europe in recent years.

In the ranks, these journalists have more to contend with as professionals than in times past, and less support. There's more adversity on the job that drives too many of them at midcareer away from the news business with an acid view of the course it's on. Most of that is owing to decisions by those in overall charge of news organizations, adding to sourness down the line.

It was hardly a secret in the newsroom that the retrenchment that news business executives put their workforces through in the early '90s, fiercer than anything since that forced by World War II rationing, was dictated at least as much by the imperative to meet profit margin goals for the benefit of Wall Street as by the overall marketplace crisis of the news business. In previous decades, enduring hard times would have been a matter of rolling with the punch, and coming back from it with fresh initiative and investment. This time the layoffs and buyouts, the closing down of regional, national, and foreign bureaus and shrinking of news budgets and space also closed down an era of expansive thinking in the industry, without ceremony. News organizations' acquiescence in the perceived shutdown of public interest in a wider world out there, and their reflex of looking more to their marketing departments than to their news departments for wisdom, had their inevitable effect on the aspirations of journalism's best and brightest.

And for the stalwart professionals in the newsroom and in the field, often fighting like partisans in the hills against the occupying forces of bottom-line management, the achievement of good work was ever more challenged by the cutbacks and cost cutting. The newsmagazines downsized their fact-checking forces, in favor of flash. The networks shut the doors on many of their foreign bureaus. Newspapers let critical vacated positions go unfilled, shrank newsholes, slashed national and foreign coverage in favor of the local front, rationalizing cost cutting with survey data about lack of reader interest beyond home. Depth, breadth, and authority of coverage suffered.[1]

AND YET, WITH little or no help from those in ultimate charge, there were positive indicators now and then in the business, and evidence that the good fight was still worth fighting. At the command-post level, Gene Roberts's departure from the editorship of The Philadelphia Inquirer in 1990 was bad news for the journalistic profession. His return to newspapering in 1993 in the number-two newsroom position at The New York Times brought that paper's news staff a leader with an unusual knack for seeing the forest as well as the trees. At the Inquirer, Roberts had prompted critical, probing inquiries into the effects of government policy on working people in the Reagan and Bush years. The *Times*'s stand-back, critical interpretation of such trends as corporate downsizing and urban decay under Roberts's influence were exceptions to the rule that most American news organizations have neglected the most profound and troubling aspects of the story of our time.[2]

In 1997 and 1998, the *Times* and *The Wall Street Journal* also broke the lock of retrenchment, reinvesting once again in "product" under improved economic conditions. Seeking to build on their success with their national editions, each added significant space for expanded coverage of topics including arts and culture, technology, science, and medicine. Pitifully few other news organizations, such as *The Dallas Morning News,* fed resources back into newspapering, exceptions to the new rule that such funding is for the chimera of "new media."[3]

The New York Times, other papers are fond of saying, is in a class by itself; therefore, others should not be held to its standards. In fact, the Pulitzer Prize jurors and other award committees still consume as many (and more) arduous hours choosing from among as much (and more) work of truly original enterprise and quality emerging from scores of news organizations other than *The New York Times* as they did five years ago. Journalists of talent, courage, and the gift of critical thinking labor on in an industry that, at the top, has lost its way.[4]

SO WE ARRIVE at a station where the majority of the leaders of a profession and an industry persuade themselves in desperation to purge themselves of the qualities that made them great.

The foot soldiers of the press labor on. Its leaders are inclined to turn their backs on journalism's magic — unpredictability and serendipity; odd collisions of events in time, of subject and writer, of conventional wisdom and its upset; above all, the play of instinct. Their new concerns are with "research," known preference, safe choice, customer service, formula. The journalist as explorer and adventurer, as artist and soldier of fortune, as shaman unearthing a disturbing secret of relevance to the public, is up on charges of elitism and arrogance. The idea is to trade in the old street wisdom for the role of community "information worker" for consumers who may or may not want the product in question. The idea is to push journalistic professionalism in all its range of possibility and adventure in the direction of robotics.

Meanwhile the trend among the industry's business executives is to align themselves with the marketing cult of segmentation and targeting. In doing so they feed a trend that erodes social and political commonality and therefore the value of news and information for broad audiences. The industry has indeed suffered multiple catastrophes. It has also worked overtime to make them worse.

THE CHARGE OF elitism leveled against the press from within and without, the indictment for presuming to make judgments on behalf of audiences, is misdirected. The real problem, the very devil, is the fragmentation of society and the disintegration of political culture. Add to that the ascendancy of the corporate profit imperative in the news business, which demands of the press that instead of considering the argument for combating social fragmentation, it figure out how to profit from it.

The American press won't regain its bearings, the news business won't regain its purchase on the present or future, by fiddling with "consumer-driven models" or "niching" or twenty-first-century graphics or "repackaging" or computer technology or any other secondary device for reaching readers and viewers. The press will continue to lose ground as long as its core product — news — fails to engage people beyond the level of the sensational, the frivolous, and the merely selfish. And the news will fail to engage people profoundly, and, worse, will alienate them, as long as social fragmentation pulls them away from a common engagement with the news, and as long as government and politics in our country remain what they've become: ineffective, degraded, debased, despised, incompetent to deal with society's real and deep problems, and irrelevant to so many millions of Americans.

WHAT THEN is to be done?

It's unrealistic to exhort journalism to fill the vacant space that only a vibrant, rooted, functioning politics can fill. It's beside the point to attack journalism for making matters worse when, instinctively, it functions as a watchdog to a corrupted political structure.

It's a form of national blindness to avoid the paramount issues in the land — political and governmental dysfunction, economic polarization, deepening racial division and resegregation, cultural disintegration — and to find solace, as the nation did for most of the 1990s, in cyber-recreation and passing boom times.

Journalism cannot solve these problems however empowered or wise in a "civic" role it might become. Nor can American politics in its current sorry shape.

The prime players in the news business itself are trapped in the various structural conditions that underlie it — newspapers in their metropolitan geographic franchise, television in its visual and entertainment imperatives, the mass market newsmagazines in their growing market irrelevance. Their maneuverability is in many ways limited to the kinds of devices, mechanical and cosmetic, they've tried to stanch their losses with thus far. Even so, their lack of truly imaginative, radical impulse in the face of so much trouble is striking. Was there, is there a realistic business scenario for easing news organizations out from under the tyranny of small-minded Wall Street analysts? The subject doesn't even get raised.

WHAT THEN is to be done?

For some years discussion of the degradation of public life has focused on Carlylean themes, in essays with titles like "Where Have All the Heroes Gone?" Now and then a political leader has seemed tempted to seek center stage, promising a language that doesn't lie about our common lot. But the notion of breaking out of the games second-guessed by pollsters and political consultants, the games of image management and media strategy, has, it seems, become a prohibitively expensive form of idealism, given the cost of a national campaign. The notion lingers. Every four years an independent-minded presidential hopeful toys with it. As in the case of the late Morris Udall, it is mentioned in their obituaries.

What could the press do to force the issue? For the most part, responsible journalists don't know any code other than to press on re-gardless. Holding to high standards of professionalism was, for many decades, doing what came naturally. The acceleration of front-office pressures to be more profit minded and more marketing minded have had the effect of rendering journalism's professional code that much more daring and heroic. Formerly distinguished news organizations like *The Atlanta Journal-Constitution, The Miami Herald,* the news-magazines, and television news divisions that have taken themselves even part way down the formulaic marketing path have in effect stigmatized themselves professionally, and most of those who run them and work for them know it. Papers like *The New York Times* and *The Philadelphia Inquirer* that have labored to hold the line stand taller. There are obvious compensations for those who run and work for the latter.

But the compensations have their limits. Everywhere the profit and marketing pressures are at odds with journalism's professional identity; everywhere journalists are called upon to do more with less. And everywhere that state of affairs takes a toll on morale. Good journalists gain a reputation — and leave the business (but not neces-sarily their calling; a number leave to write books).[5]

The remedies that can be applied are limited, defensive, and rela-tively obvious. Some news organizations have learned the hard way how crucial it is to protect their credibility. *The Washington Post* (in the case of reporter Janet Cooke), the *San Jose Mercury News* (in the case of allegations of CIA involvement in drug traffic), *The Boston Globe* (in the cases of columnists Patricia Smith and Mike Barnicle), *Time* and CNN (in the case of alleged U.S. military use of nerve gas in Vietnam) all forced themselves through humiliating public cleans-ings in recent years when confronted with make-believe or exaggera-tion on the part of reporters and writers in their employ. The price to all concerned was high. But internally and to outsiders, these epi-sodes served as vivid reminders of the rules of journalism, the rea-sons for them, the price that top managers still attach to them, and audiences' interest in knowing that faith is kept with them.

But when day is done the demands of the marketplace on the press are ever more inexorable. Jack Fuller, publisher and former editor of the *Chicago Tribune* and one of the exceptions to the general rule that news business leaders today are not original thinkers, has put the situation of newspapers in the modern corporate context in the most clinical of analytic terms — and flipped a coin:

> If one thinks that newspapers are slowly but inevitably dying, that people's tastes have shifted irretrievably against them, then one would make only very modest investments to keep the enterprise running as it winds down, drawing as much cash as possible from it in order to grow in other areas. On the other hand, if one thinks that newspapers are poised for renewal, that the road ahead seems built for them, then the projected return on investments would be higher than under the pessimistic assumption, the risk would be lower, and it would make excellent sense to put money into the enterprise to position it for takeoff.

Arguing that "news values" and profitability are compatible if newspapers labor to "fit into the new, fragmented information environment," Fuller, as a publisher and manager, put his carefully worded challenge to his former colleagues in the newsroom this way: "If good journalists look on this medium with hostility or treat it as suited only for vapid entertainment, then it will be no wonder if investors decide that papers have no future. But if journalists put their minds to the task of translating news values and moving customers into the new modes of reaching the audience, they will make investment in what they do much more attractive."[6]

Fuller's formulation, like so much else written about the press in recent years, keeps the discussion within the frame of the profession and the business, apart from the spheres where the news itself is generated. Rightly, he suggests that news organizations that put themselves through coherent thought processes are capable of making rational choices about their professional missions, as distinct from imposing mindless cost cutting or faddish journalistic formulas in search of short-term profits. Such a course, like that of accepting audience erosion as the price of maintaining journalistic standards in these times, will do as a defensive strategy if supported by sound management. But it fails to come to terms with the issue of the alienation of audiences, the erosion of the relevance of the news for them — the darker parts of the story of our time.

THERE IS ANOTHER, more radical scenario; one that argues that conditions cannot improve before they get worse. That is (this argument goes), for all that's to be deplored about those conditions, they don't constitute a state of breakdown sufficient to prompt meaningful remedy.

The conditions that make "revolutionary reform," in Yale law professor Bruce Ackerman's words, both possible and necessary include the requirement that "would-be reformers . . . earn huge quantities of institutional credibility before they gain higher lawmaking recognition" — that is, before they may gain a hearing for extraordinary measures. That does not happen in the case of mere malaise.[7]

Our nation has passed through times when the system did break down, and when radical action to remedy the situation could no longer be denied. The most dramatic of them were in the crisis years of the Civil War and the Great Depression, when obsolete cultural and social as well as political and economic assumptions were retired absolutely and new ones adopted. Ackerman, an authority on both those epic experiences, sees such "signs of dissatisfaction [today] . . . and an increasing tendency to search for structural change."[8]

There are comparable analyses on the part of sociologist Amitai Etzioni and his "communitarian movement" colleagues, and by some advocates of radical constitutional revision. The latter, concerned about governmental paralysis and political disintegration, see a need for fundamental readjustments to our Constitution. That Constitution, as one of them, Daniel Lazare, has written, suspends "the three branches of government . . . in almost perfect equipoise" — an equipoise that has helped to foster the governmental gridlock of recent years, and to frustrate the kinds of action required to meet societal challenges unimaginable to the good men of the eighteenth century who designed the Constitution.[9]

And there are proposals for a radical overhaul of our absurd presidential campaign system, including drastically shortening it. In *Buckley v. Valeo* (1976), the Supreme Court leaned on the First

Amendment to lock the power of money (and, effectively, negative political advertising on television) into late-twentieth-century election campaigns. One day, perhaps, as in the Progressive and New Deal eras, such reasoning will be seen to be as perverse as that of the Robber Baron–era doctrinaires who twisted the post–Civil War Reconstruction's Fourteenth Amendment into a sanctification of the corporation as a "person" entitled to freedom from regulation.[10]

The scope of this book does not leave room for review of those discussions in detail. I mention them to suggest that, as with them, not much is likely to come of the analysis and arguments presented here as a simple matter of course or logic. The powers of inertia at work today are too persistent to permit meaningful reform. The dysfunctions they carry aren't toxic enough to force it. The combination of social, cultural, and political disintegration with homiletic, ineffectual "mediating" communication about it adds up to a set of organized dysfunctions, short of anarchy. The result is that there's little to fear, or hope for, except more of the same. We are a republic of denial.

WHAT WOULD CONSTITUTE a basis for change, action, reconstitution?

A crisis that stopped the nation cold? Failure to elect a president from a fragmented field and a stalemated electoral process? A combination of economic collapse, or sociopolitical anarchy, and governmental paralysis in the face of that? Some of those were aspects of the crises of 1860–61 and 1933.

The nation was blessed on both those occasions with newly elected presidents gifted with extraordinary political instincts and abilities. As noted earlier, one of Lincoln's and Roosevelt's most opaque and fascinating shared attributes was the extent to which they were at once self-directed and restrained, and traveled essentially alone. They employed no organized apparatuses of opinion research or manipulation; they relied on informal communication and their own innate strengths and wiles. They had the advantage of raw, underused, and supple governing structures. They found ways to mobilize swiftly what meager structure there was, and to exploit its meagerness as a justification for emergency powers.

Those are hardly the conditions of today's political environment. A modern crisis of nationhood, society, and governance is likely to be less contained or coherent than were those of 1861 or 1933. In the first one, a clear-cut civil war along regional lines was a reality; in the second, one nearly as clear-cut along class lines was in the air.

A modern "national emergency government" on the European model, martial law, a call for a constitutional convention (which would, it is argued, quickly clip the First Amendment protections of the press), would be the tamest imaginable early consequences. Then factor in the mobility and volatility of modern life compared with 1933 or 1861; factor in modern terrorism and technology in combination with the ancient force of anarchy, all loose in a paralyzed United States. These are story lines with which the most exploitative of modern communications media, the entertainment industry, has been toying for some time.

What is the point in engaging in such doomsday play? It's not to point the accusing finger, but rather to suggest that the forest is vast and dark, and that we are in it with no clear path out. Were politics for its part, or journalism for its, able to organize engaged debate about these issues leading to effective action, there would be no need to suggest so somber a picture. But so far, they can't.

Notes

Introduction: A Story of Our Time

1. *Blood, Toil, Tears, and Sweat: The Speeches of Winston Churchill,* edited by David Cannadine (Houghton Mifflin, Boston, 1989), p. 11; *I Can Hear It Now: Winston Churchill,* Columbia Masterworks recording ML 5056, edited by Edward R. Murrow and Fred W. Friendly with narration by Edward R. Murrow; William Allen White, *The Autobiography of William Allen White* (Macmillan, New York, 1946), p. 648.

2. David Brinkley, *Washington Goes to War* (Knopf, New York, 1988), p. 171.

3. Theodore J. Lowi, *The End of Liberalism: The Second Republic of the United States* (Norton, New York, 1979), pp. xii, 313; Michael J. Sandel, *Democracy's Discontent: America in Search of a Public Philosophy* (Harvard University Press, Cambridge, 1996), p. 294; E. J. Dionne, *Why Americans Hate Politics* (Touchstone, New York, 1992), p. 10; Arthur M. Schlesinger, Jr., *The Disuniting of America: Reflections on a Multicultural Society* (Norton, New York, 1992), p. 41.

4. Thomas E. Patterson, *Out of Order* (Knopf, New York, 1993); Larry J. Sabato, *Feeding Frenzy: How Attack Journalism Has Transformed American Politics* (Free Press, New York, 1991), pp. 1, 23; Suzanne Garment, *Scandal: The Culture of Mistrust in American Politics* (Times Books, New York, 1991), p. 82.

5. Broder is quoted in Joseph Capella and Kathleen Hall Jamieson, *The Spiral of Cynicism: The Press and the Public Good* (Oxford University Press, New York, 1997), p. 17; James Fallows, *Breaking the News: How the Media Undermine American Democracy* (Pantheon, New York, 1996), p. 9.

6. A note on usage: I'm going to forgo for the most part the unlovely verbiage "news media" and run with the gutsier "press." We employ "news media" as a means of updating the print-and-ink-tinged "press," thereby recognizing radio, television, and now the Internet.

But "press" also connotes a process—journalism—and not simply a channel. Much of the news on the air is written before it's spoken. Washington journalists in all media continue to deal with the White House press secretary and the State Department press office. The First Amendment to the Constitution speaks of the press, and so for now shall I. When referring to the press as an industry, I'll generally speak of the news business.

7. Katherine Q. Seelye, "Voters Disgusted with Politicians as Election Nears," *New York Times,* November 3, 1994, p. A1; Richard Morin and Dan Balz, "Americans Losing Trust in Each Other and Institutions," *Washington Post,* January 28, 1996, p. A1; Robert D. Putnam, "The Strange Disappearance of Civic America," *American Prospect,* winter 1996, pp. 34–48; "The Optimism Gap Grows," publication of the Pew Research Center for the People and the Press, January 17, 1997; Gerald F. Seib, "Many Americans View Washington as a Mess and Just Tune It Out," *Wall Street Journal,* June 4, 1997, p. A1.

8. Walter Lippmann, *Liberty and the News* (Harcourt Brace and Hone, New York, 1920), p. 5.

9. Howard Kurtz, "*Time* Pulls Clinton 'Scoop'; Executives Apologize for Internet Report," *Washington Post,* August 15, 1998, p. B3; Maureen Dowd, "Doomsday Strategy," *New York Times,* February 11, 1998, p. A29.

10. Putnam, "The Strange Disappearance of Civic America," p. 46; Michael Schudson, "What If Civic Life Didn't Die?" Theda Skocpol, "Unravelling from Above," and response by Robert Putnam, all in *American Prospect,* March–April 1996, pp. 17, 20, 26.

Chapter 1: "Let's Remember the Energy"

1. Henry R. Luce, *The American Century* (Farrar & Rinehart, New York, 1941), pp. 23, 32–33.

2. Donald W. White, *The American Century: The Rise and Decline of the United States as a World Power* (Yale University Press, New Haven, 1997), p. 85.

3. Alan Brinkley, *The End of Reform: New Deal Liberalism in Recession and War* (Knopf, New York, 1995), pp. 260–64, 269–71.

4. Nelson Lichtenstein, *The Most Dangerous Man in Detroit: Walter Reuther and the Fate of American Labor* (Basic Books, New York, 1995), pp. 207–11, 224–26; Brinkley, *The End of Reform,* pp. 166–70; Alonzo L. Hamby, *Man of the People: A Life of Harry S. Truman* (Oxford University Press, New York, 1995), pp. 364–65, 433–35.

5. Philip Roth, *American Pastoral* (Houghton Mifflin, Boston, 1997), pp. 40–41.

6. Dean G. Acheson, *Present at the Creation: My Years at the State Department* (Norton, New York, 1969), p. 727.

7. E. B. White, *New Yorker,* May 12, 1945, quoted in *Reporting World War II,* vol. 2, *American Journalism, 1944–1945* (Library of America, New York, 1995), pp. 752–53.

8. Sidney Blumenthal, "Lippmann's Cave," paper delivered at Bard College at centennial celebration for Walter Lippmann, September 28, 1989.

9. James Chace, *Dean Acheson* (Simon & Schuster, New York, 1998), p. 199; James Reston, *Deadline: A Memoir* (Random House, New York, 1991), pp. 145–46.

10. For Luce and Churchill, see W. A. Swanburg, *Luce and His Empire* (Charles Scribner's Sons, New York, 1972), p. 278. For the Philip Graham–Clark Clifford anecdote, see Ben Bradlee, *A Good Life: Newspapering and Other Adventures* (Simon & Schuster, New York, 1995), pp. 127–28; Katharine Graham, *Personal History* (Knopf, New York, 1997), p. 186.

11. Edwin R. Bayley, *Joe McCarthy and the Press* (University of Wisconsin Press, Madison, 1981), pp. 3–4, 67–70.

12. Chace, *Dean Acheson*, p. 240.

13. C. Wright Mills, *The Causes of World War Three* (Simon & Schuster, New York, 1958), p. 2.

14. For the congressional defeat of the legislation to overturn liberal Supreme Court decisions, see Robert Dallek, *Lone Star Rising: Lyndon Johnson and His Times* (Oxford University Press, New York, 1991), pp. 535–36.

15. For an informed discussion of the "tacit approval" by Senator Russell of passage of the 1957 Civil Rights Act, see Robert Mann, *The Walls of Jericho: Lyndon Johnson, Hubert Humphrey, Richard Russell, and the Struggle for Civil Rights* (Harcourt Brace, New York, 1996), pp. 191–224.

16. White, *The American Century*, pp. 78–85, 124–26.

17. Meg Greenfield, "The Problem Problem," *Reporter*, February 25, 1965, pp. 31–32.

Chapter 2: And Then . . .

1. Paul Jacobs and Saul Landau, *The New Radicals* (Vintage, New York, 1966), pp. 152–53.

2. Irving Bernstein, *Guns or Butter: The Presidency of Lyndon Johnson* (Oxford University Press, New York, 1996), p. 381; "15,000 White House Pickets Denounce Vietnam War," *New York Times*, April 18, 1965, p. 1.

3. E. W. Kenworthy, "Kennedy Warns Buddhist Dispute Imperils Vietnam," *New York Times*, September 3, 1963.

4. Seymour Topping, "Frustration in Vietnam," *New York Times*, March 10, 1964, p. 3; Peter Grose, "McNamara Said to Favor Harassing North Vietnam," *New York Times*, March 14, 1964, p. 1, Jack Raymond, "McNamara Tells Johnson of Gain in Vietnam War," *New York Times*, March 15, 1964, p. 1; "U.S. to Add $50 Million to Yearly Aid for Saigon," *New York Times*, March 30, 1964, p. 1.

5. David Halberstam, *The Making of a Quagmire* (Random House, New

York, 1964), p. 72; Philip Knightly, *The First Casualty* (Harcourt Brace Jovanovich, New York, 1975), pp. 376, 380.

6. Jacobs and Landau, *The New Radicals*, p. 151; Todd Gitlin, *The Sixties: Years of Hope, Days of Rage* (Bantam Books, New York, 1987), pp. 31–32.

7. Lewis Chester, Godfrey Hodgson, and Bruce Page, *An American Melodrama: The Presidential Campaign of 1968* (Viking, New York, 1969), pp. 582, 592, 597; Jules Witcover, *The Year the Dream Died: Revisiting 1968 in America* (Warner Books, New York, 1997), pp. 333–35.

8. Thomas Byrne Edsall and Mary D. Edsall, *Chain Reaction: The Impact of Race, Rights, and Taxes on American Politics* (Norton, New York, 1991), pp. 58–59.

9. Michael Schudson, *Watergate in American Memory* (Basic Books, New York, 1992), pp. 41–43, 90.

10. Michael Schudson, *The Good Citizen: A History of American Civic Life* (Free Press, New York, 1998), p. 191; Thomas Patterson, *Out of Order* (Knopf, New York, 1993), pp. 30–32; Edsall and Edsall, *Chain Reaction,* pp. 91–94.

11. Edsall and Edsall, *Chain Reaction,* pp. 93–94.

12. Paul Allen Beck and Frank J. Sorauf, *Party Politics in America,* 7th ed. (HarperCollins, New York, 1992), pp. 458–59; Dionne, *Why Americans Hate Politics,* p. 204.

13. White, *The American Century,* p. 385.

14. Ibid., p. 389.

15. Ibid., pp. 395–97; *Life,* September 1, 1972, cover and pp. 30–38.

16. Fred Siegel, *The Future Once Happened Here: New York, D.C., L.A., and the Fate of America's Big Cities* (Free Press, New York, 1997), pp. ix, 201; Nicholas Lemann, *The Promised Land: The Great Black Migration and How It Changed America* (Knopf, New York, 1991), pp. 140–45, 196–202, 344–45.

17. White, *The American Century,* 384–95, 403.

18. Richard McGowan, *State Lotteries and Legalized Gambling: Painless Revenue or Painful Mirage* (Quorum Books, Westport, Conn., 1994), pp. 9–20; James Cook, "Lottomania," *Forbes,* March 6, 1989, p. 92; William B. Falk, "The $482B Jackpot," *Newsday,* December 3, 1995, p. A4; Robert Goodman, *The Luck Business* (Free Press, New York, 1995), pp. 126–28, 163–64; Ford Fessenden and John Riley, "And the Poor Get Poorer," *Newsday,* December 4, 1995, p. A7.

19. Edsall and Edsall, *Chain Reaction,* pp. 280–81.

20. Patterson, *Out of Order,* p. 34.

21. Everett Carll Ladd, Jr., *Where Have All the Voters Gone? The Fracturing of America's Political Parties* (Norton, New York, 1978), pp. 35–36; Neil Postman, *Amusing Ourselves to Death: Public Discourse in the Age of Show Business* (Viking Penguin, New York, 1985), p. 87; Kevin Sack,

"From Sea to Shining Sea, the TV Campaign Is All Attack Ads, All the Time," *New York Times,* October 30, 1998, p. A31.

Chapter 3: Malaise

1. Robert Christopher, "Why Are We in Vietnam?" *Newsweek,* November 27, 1967, p. 37.

2. George Ball, *The Past Has Another Pattern: Memoirs* (Norton, New York, 1982), p. 378.

3. "Vietnam Aftermath," *New York Times,* January 26, 1973, p. 34.

4. Robert Stobaugh and Daniel Yergin, editors, *Energy Future: Report of the Harvard Business School Energy Project* (Random House, New York, 1979), pp. 4, 216–33; "On Reaching a State of Global Equilibrium," *New York Times,* March 13, 1972, p. 35; *Newsweek* covers, July 9 and November 26, 1979.

5. "Transcript of President's Address on Moves to Deal with Economic Problems," *New York Times,* August 16, 1971, p. 14; White, *The American Century,* p. 341.

6. For "post-Vietnam syndrome," see for example Philip Geyelin, "Flailing About Foreign Policy," *Washington Post,* September 11, 1980, p. A19.

7. Siegel, *The Future Once Happened Here,* pp. xii, 44.

8. "In the early seventies," wrote FitzGerald, "there had been five large interconnected communes on the southern border of Vermont engaged variously in New Left politics, subsistence farming, community Shakespeare, gay and feminist consciousness-raising, and cooking with, or smoking, fresh herbs." Frances FitzGerald, *Cities on a Hill: A Journey Through Contemporary American Cultures* (Simon & Schuster, New York, 1986), pp. 21, 387, 390–91, 414.

9. Martin Schram, "Carter: Back on Track and Eager to Retake the Lead," *Washington Post,* July 17, 1979; Sidney Blumenthal, *The Permanent Campaign* (Beacon Press, Boston, 1980), p. 54; Christopher Lasch, *The Culture of Narcissism: American Life in an Age of Diminishing Expectations* (Norton, New York, 1978), p. 218.

10. Hendrik Hertzberg, interview by author, July 22, 1998; Adam Clymer, "Republicans Call Energy Speech Political and Vague," *New York Times,* July 16, 1979, p. A11; Adam Clymer, "Politicians Divided Along Party Lines Over the President's Energy Address," *New York Times,* July 17, 1979, p. A12; "Transcript of President's Address to Country on Energy Problems," *New York Times,* July 16, 1979, p. A10.

11. Sandel, *Democracy's Discontent,* pp. 346, 297.

12. "They Have to Listen Now," *Newsweek,* March 27, 1972, p. 24; "Interview with George Wallace," *U.S. News & World Report,* June 15, 1970, p. 24.

13. " 'Welfare Queen' Becomes Issue in Reagan Campaign," *New York Times,* February 15, 1976, p. A51; Harry C. McPherson, *A Political Education: A Washington Memoir* (Houghton Mifflin, Boston, 1988), p. 477; Michael Janeway, "So Who Is Michael Dukakis?" *New England Monthly,* December 1987, pp. 72, 128.

14. Figures supplied by Election Data Services, Washington, D.C.

15. Newspaper Association of America, "Keys to Our Survival," a Joint Project of the ASNE 1990–91 Readership and Research and 1991 Future of Newspapers Committees, American Society of Newspaper Editors Foundation.

16. Alex S. Jones, "For News Magazines, Growing Identity Crisis," *New York Times,* June 29, 1988, p. C26.

17. Nielsen Media Research, ratings and share for early evening news (full season average).

18. Richard Ford, *Independence Day* (Knopf, New York, 1995), pp. 4–5, 10.

19. Among the twelve symptoms of depressive behavior listed in the *Diagnostic and Statistical Manual of Mental Disorders,* 4th ed. (DSM-4), are:

2. low energy or chronic fatigue
3. feelings of inadequacy
4. decreased effectiveness or productivity at school, work, or home
5. decreased attention, concentration, or ability to think clearly
6. social withdrawal
8. restriction of involvement in pleasurable activities; guilt over past activities
9. feeling slowed down
11. pessimistic attitude towards the future, or brooding about past events.

Sometimes associated with depression are "hypomanic" interludes between depressive ones. The DSM-4's list of symptoms for such behavior, parallel to the list of depressive symptoms, includes

3. inflated self-esteem
4. increased productivity, often associated with unusual and self-imposed working hours
5. sharpened and unusually creative thinking
7. hypersexuality without recognition of possibility of painful consequences
8. excessive involvement in pleasurable activities with lack of concern for the high potential for painful consequences, e.g., buying sprees, foolish business investments . . .
11. overoptimism or exaggeration of past achievements.

Not to make more of these analytic measurements than is warranted, nor to practice unlicensed psychiatry on a mass scale, it's possible to say that the two lists are at least suggestive in trying to make coherent sense of the events, taken together, described in earlier pages, their effects on Americans individually and collectively, and representation of them in quantified form in surveys of the mood of the nation.

The first list tracks with the national "post-Vietnam syndrome," with the demoralizing "rustbelt" effect, and with survey research on public hopes and fears. The second list tracks with aspects of "me generation" and yuppie culture, and with other generational detritus: 1980s sexual hedonism preceding the onset of the AIDS epidemic; the "morning in America" rhetoric of the Reagan administration; the titanic, often messianic claims of the new moguls of the cybernetics, communications, and entertainment industries, and of cult leaders and New Age gurus.

Chapter 4: Structure

1. Alan Brinkley, "The Privatization of Public Discourse," in Alan Brinkley, Nelson W. Polsby, and Kathleen M. Sullivan, *New Federalist Papers* (Norton, New York, 1997), p. 127.

2. Steven A. Holmes, "Gun Control Politics Is Most Local of All," *New York Times*, April 14, 1991, section 4, p. 5; Dan Balz, "Urban Violence Is Changing the Politics of Gun Control," *Washington Post*, October 18, 1993, p. A1; David E. Rosenbaum, "The Gun Minority Flexes Muscle," *New York Times*, May 5, 1994, p. B10; Erik Eckholm, "Thorny Issue on Gun Control: Curbing Responsible Owners," *New York Times*, April 3, 1992, p. A1; "Gunfire Shatters Peace and Lives in Washington," *New York Times*, June 11, 1992, p. B10; "Study Links Rise in Killings to Relaxed Gun Laws," *New York Times*, March 15, 1985, p. A23.

For a pungent discussion of the problems in contemplating reform of such representational inequity in the Senate in the face of the requirements of Article 5 of the Constitution, see Daniel Lazare, *The Frozen Republic: How the Constitution Is Paralyzing Democracy* (Harcourt Brace, New York, 1996), pp. 157–62, 182–84.

3. Martin P. Wattenberg, *The Decline of American Political Parties, 1952–1980* (Harvard University Press, Cambridge, 1984), p. xv; John H. Aldrich, *Why Parties? The Origin and Transformation of Political Parties in America* (University of Chicago Press, Chicago, 1995), p. 241. Walter Dean Burnham, who contributed a foreword to Wattenberg's book, is the author of the third quotation; Burnham quotes Giobanni Sartori, author of the fourth quotation.

4. Aldrich, *Why Parties?* pp. 9–10.

5. Ibid., pp. 8–9; Wattenberg, *The Decline of American Parties*, pp. 128–29.

6. Beck and Sorauf, *Party Politics in America*, pp. 429, 471; Aldrich, *Why Parties?* pp. 244–45, 272; Wattenberg, *The Decline of American Parties*, p. 109; Jill Abramson, "The Business of Persuasion Thrives in Nation's Capital," *New York Times*, September 29, 1998, p. A1.

7. Elaine Ciulla Karmack and William Galston, "The Politics of Evasion: Democrats and the Presidency," paper issued by the Progressive Policy Institute, Washington, D.C., September 1989, pp. 3, 7, 16; Schudson, *The Good Citizen*, pp. 275–76; Dionne, *Why Americans Hate Politics*, pp. 121–24, 136–37; 370–72; Edsall and Edsall, *Chain Reaction*, pp. 193–95, 198, 201; "The New Political Landscape," publication of the Times Mirror Center for the People and the Press, October 1994, pp. 7–8.

8. Beck and Sorauf, *Party Politics in America*, pp. 457–58; Blumenthal, *The Permanent Campaign*, pp. 7–9.

9. Richard Wirthlin, foreword to Frank I. Luntz, *Candidates, Consultants, and Campaigns: The Style and Substance of American Electioneering* (Basil Blackwell, London, 1988), p. vii.

10. Luntz, *Candidates, Consultants, and Campaigns*, pp. 6–12, 168–71, 183–85; Patterson, *Out of Order*, p. 32.

11. Michael Schudson, *The Power of News* (Harvard University Press, Cambridge, 1995), p. 24; Putnam, "The Strange Disappearance of Civic America," p. 46.

12. Frank Sorauf quoted in Wattenberg, *The Decline of American Parties*, p. 91; Wattenberg, *The Decline of American Parties*, p. 126; Postman, *Amusing Ourselves to Death*, p. 97.

13. Wattenberg, *The Decline of American Parties*, pp. 128–29.

14. Harry McPherson, interview by author, December 18, 1994; Ann Richards to author, January 30, 1996.

15. Luntz, *Candidates, Consultants, and Campaigns*, p. 69; Sack, "From Sea to Shining Sea."

16. Under *Herbert v. Lando*, libel plaintiffs won the right to "discover" what's in a journalist's raw notes, files, and outtakes. See Rodney A. Smolla, *Suing the Press: Libel, the Media, and Power* (Oxford University Press, New York, 1986), pp. 68–71.

17. A search of the Vanderbilt University Television News Archive reveals ninety-three "War on Drugs" stories on NBC News between 1988 and 1992.

18. Marvin Kalb, director of the Shorenstein Center for Press, Politics, and Public Policy at Harvard University's Kennedy School of Government, interview by author, October 1, 1998.

19. Jonathan Alter, "Clinton in the Twilight Zone," *Newsweek*, June 15, 1992, p. 28.

20. Michael J. Arlen, *The View from Highway 1* (Farrar, Straus & Giroux, New York, 1976), pp. 126, 129, 160.

21. A word about the academic argument whether television coverage played a causal role in the turning of the American public against the Vietnam War is in order.

The tendency of some social scientists has been to focus on content analysis of television coverage of the Vietnam War to demonstrate that it was far from being critical until very late in the game; and then to conclude, focusing on polling and survey data, that the effect of the coverage on declining support for the war was minimal. See, for example, Daniel C. Hallin, *"The Uncensored War": The Media and Vietnam* (Oxford University Press, New York, 1986), pp. 129–34, 212–13. A more sophisticated essay is Michael Mandelbaum's "Vietnam: The Television War," *Daedalus,* fall 1982, pp. 157–69.

Such conclusions are in my view misguided in framing the question of television's role in a relative vacuum, rather than considering the war and all its cumulative effects on domestic public opinion in the larger social, cultural, and news environment of the 1960s. My purpose on this point, as with this book as a whole, is to suggest that a full understanding of the processes at work since the 1960s is best served by expanding the focus. They're ill served by narrowing in with overly literal interpretations of survey data about issues that are, as Vietnam most especially was before opposition to it became widespread, fraught with conflict and pain. The confusion in opinion on such issues defies linear analysis, and again and again — as in the first months of 1968 — topples political reasoning based on such analysis.

To give just one example of what's lost by compartmentalizing the question to that of television's role alone, print news media published much more explicit and disturbing photos of wounded and dead American men in combat during the Vietnam War than they had in previous conflicts. Those pictures in turn played into the consciousness of people absorbing the vague words and images on television about a war without apparent boundaries or clear goals or end. As early as 1966 *Life* ran unusually vivid cover photos and inside spreads of such casualties. Late in 1967 I asked then senator Eugene McCarthy in an interview what voters were giving him as specific reasons for erosion of their support for the war. He replied, "All those pictures of wounded GIs in *Life.*" (See, for example, "The War Goes On," photographed by Henri Huet, *Life,* February 11, 1966, cover and pp. 20–24; "Invasion DMZ Runs into the Marines," photographed by Larry Burrows and Co Rentmeester, *Life,* October 28, 1966, cover and pp. 30–39; and "The Battle That Required and Ruined Hue," photographed by John Olson, *Life,* March 8, 1968, pp. 25–29.) In fact, those pictures were part of a larger shift in consciousness of which television and its portrayals of the nature of the war in the field, and growing opposition and doubt about it at home, were an enormous, and fluid, part.

To suggest another way of considering the question, support for the Vietnam War fell away in the context of a decade of violence and anti-establishment protest of various kinds, heavily covered by television in its march to preeminence over print as the public's principal source of news, all of which contributed to a souring of the overall public mood. In all respects, such was not the case in the World War II or Korean War years.

22. Sissela Bok, *Mayhem* (Addison-Wesley, Reading, Mass., 1998), p. 3.

23. Don DeLillo, *Underworld* (Scribner, New York, 1997), pp. 159–60.

24. Michael Oreskes, "America's Politics Loses Way as Its Vision Changes World," *New York Times*, March 18, 1990, p. A1.

25. Paul Weaver, "Is Television News Biased?" *Public Interest*, winter 1972, p. 67.

26. Abramson, "The Business of Persuasion Thrives in the Nation's Capital"; Alison Mitchell, "A New Form of Lobbying Puts a Public Face on Private Interest," *New York Times*, September 30, 1998, p. A1.

27. Alison Mitchell, "Frustrated with the President, but a First Line of Defense," *New York Times*, October 4, 1998, p. A26.

28. Alison Mitchell, "Outlook for Political Dynamics: More of the Same," *New York Times*, October 22, 1998, p. A25; Sack, "From Sea to Shining Sea."

29. Michael M. Weinstein, "Five Problems Tarnishing a Robust Economy," *New York Times*, January 4, 1999, p. C10; Katharine Q. Seelye, "Voters Disgusted with Politicians as Election Nears," *New York Times*, November 3, 1994, p. A1.

30. Louis Uchitelle, "That Was Then and This Is the '90s," *New York Times*, June 18, 1997, p. C1; Louis Uchitelle, "Downsizing Comes Back, but the Outcry Is Muted," *New York Times*, December 7, 1998, p. A1.

31. Jason DeParle of *The New York Times* covered the "workfare" story with unusual dedication and insight. See among other pieces his "Better Work Than Welfare. But What if There's Neither?" *New York Times Magazine*, December 18, 1994, p. 44, and a follow-up report, "Welfare to Work: A Sequel," *New York Times Magazine*, December 28, 1997, p. 14.

For other late-1990s socioeconomic difficulties, see Steven Greenhouse, "Equal Work, Less-Equal Perks; Microsoft Leads the Way in Filling Jobs with 'Permatemps,'" *New York Times*, March 30, 1998, p. D1; Steven A. Holmes, "Income Disparity Between Poorest and Richest Rises," *New York Times*, June 20, 1996, p. 1; Tony Horwitz, "Some Who Lost Jobs in Early '90s Recession Find a Hard Road Back," *Wall Street Journal*, June 26, 1998, p. A1; Weinstein, "Five Problems Tarnishing a Robust Economy."

32. Louis Uchitelle, "The Middle Class: Winning in Politics, Losing in Life," *New York Times*, July 19, 1998, section 4, p. 1.

33. McGowan, *State Lotteries and Legalized Gambling*, pp. 18–20; Goodman, *The Luck Business*, pp. 126–28, 163–64; Gerri Hershey, "Gam-

bling Nation," *New York Times Magazine,* July 17, 1994, p. 36; Falk, "The $482B Jackpot"; Ford Fessenden and John Riley, "And the Poor Get Poorer," *Newsday,* December 4, 1995, p. A7; James Walsh, "Why Do People Play the Lottery?" *Consumer's Research Magazine,* March 1996, p. 22; Timothy L. O'Brien, "Gambling: Married to the Action, for Better or Worse," *New York Times,* November 8, 1998, section 4, p. 3.

34. "The Optimism Gap Grows," Pew Research Center for the People and the Press, January 17, 1997, p. 1–2.

35. Amy Harmon, "Sad, Lonely World Discovered in Cyberspace," *New York Times,* August 30, 1998, p. A1; John Sullivan, "Defendant in Internet Torture Case Gets 15 Years," *New York Times,* May 30, 1998, p. B3; Sherry Turkle, "Virtuality and Its Discontents," *American Prospect,* winter 1996, pp. 50–57; Denise Caruso, "Digital Commerce," *New York Times,* April 26, 1999, p. C4.

36. F. Scott Fitzgerald, "Echoes of the Jazz Age," in *The Crack-Up* (New Directions, New York, 1956), pp. 19–20.

37. Richard Morin and Dan Balz, "Americans Losing Trust in Each Other and Institutions," *Washington Post,* January 28, 1996, p. A1; Thomas B. Edsall, "Public Grows More Receptive to Anti-Government Message," *Washington Post,* January 31, 1996, p. A1.

38. "Whatever Happened to Politics?" articles by Gary Wills ("It's Private Lives That Matter Now"), Jacob Weisberg ("It's Stock Portfolios That Matter Now"), and Robert B. Reich ("Nothing Seems to Matter — Yet"), *New York Times Magazine,* January 25, 1998, pp. 26, 29, 32; Gerald F. Seib, "Many Americans View Washington as a Mess and Just Tune It Out," *Wall Street Journal,* June 4, 1997, p. A1.

Chapter 5: Character

1. "Fewer Favor Media Scrutiny of Political Leaders," publication by the Pew Research Center for the People and the Press, March 21, 1997, pp. 2–4; Alex S. Jones, "News Media Sharply Divided on When Right to Know Becomes Intrusion, *New York Times,* April 30, 1992, p. A11.

2. Sabato, *Feeding Frenzy,* p. 207; Garment, *Scandal,* p. 184.

3. Jones, "News Media Sharply Divided on Right to Know."

4. Joseph Alsop, *I've Seen the Best of It* (Norton, New York, 1992), pp. 388–89.

5. Anthony Lewis, *Make No Law: The Sullivan Case and the First Amendment* (Random House, New York, 1991), pp. 143, 240–44; Rodney A. Smolla, *Free Speech in an Open Society* (Knopf, New York, 1992), p. 264.

6. Lewis, *Make No Law,* pp. 158.

7. Michael Schudson, *Watergate in American Memory,* p. 20.

8. Ibid., pp. 119–20.

9. Graham, *Personal History*, pp. 420–21.

10. Joseph P. Lash, *Eleanor and Franklin* (Norton, New York, 1971), pp. 226, 237–46; Eleanor Roosevelt, *This I Remember* (Harper, New York, 1949), p. 349.

11. Michael Beschloss, *The Crisis Years: Kennedy and Khrushchev, 1960–1963* (HarperCollins, New York, 1991), pp. 138–43; Richard Reeves, *President Kennedy: Profile of Power* (Simon & Schuster, New York, 1993), pp. 288–93, 731–32, 737–38, 759; Sabato, *Feeding Frenzy*, p. 39.

12. Reeves, *President Kennedy*, pp. 290–93; Norman Mailer, "Superman Comes to the Supermarket," collected in *The Presidential Papers of Norman Mailer* (Bantam, New York, 1964), pp. 27–60.

13. Beschloss, *The Crisis Years*, pp. 189–93, 611–17.

14. Paul Taylor, *See How They Run: Electing a President in an Age of Mediaocracy* (Knopf, New York, 1990), pp. 10, 15.

15. Jack W. Germond and Jules Witcover, *Whose Broad Stripes and Bright Stars? The Trivial Pursuit of the Presidency* (Warner Books, New York, 1989), pp. 182, 191.

16. Richard Ben Cramer, *What It Takes: The Way to the White House* (Random House, New York, 1992), pp. 461, 466, 474; Taylor, *See How They Run*, p. 66; John B. Judis, "The Hart Affair," *Columbia Journalism Review*, July–August 1987, pp. 21–25; Germond and Witcover, *Whose Broad Stripes and Bright Stars?* pp. 203–9.

17. Suzanne Garment, "How Bill Clinton Got Away With It," *Wall Street Journal*, March 2, 1992; Germond and Witcover, *Whose Broad Stripes and Bright Stars?* pp. 212–13.

18. Taylor, *See How They Run*, p. 54.

19. Germond and Witcover, *Whose Broad Stripes and Bright Stars?* pp. 197–98.

20. Taylor, *See How They Run*, p. 59.

21. Quoted in Schudson, *Watergate in American Memory*, p. 163.

22. David Rosenbaum, "A Symbiosis Turned Somewhat Sour," *New York Times*, June 7, 1989, p. A25.

23. Anna Quindlen, "Journalism 2001," *New York Times*, April 12, 1992, p. A21.

24. Beschloss, *The Crisis Years*, pp. 615.

25. Alan Brinkley, "What Hart's Fall Says About America," *New York Times*, May 21, 1987, p. A31.

26. I was present at a private party in Chicago for Richard Reeves following publication of his *President Kennedy: Profile of Power* in 1993, at which Reeves described the following encounter with Clinton.

Visiting Washington on a promotional tour for the book, Reeves received an impromptu invitation to join the president and Mrs. Clinton for a brief White House visit. The presidential calendar was full, but it could be broken into at midday for a conversation over sandwiches for forty minutes or so. What the president wanted, it turned out, was for Reeves to tell him and the First Lady anecdote after anecdote about Kennedy that he'd not been able to include in his book. The forty minutes was soon up; George Stephanopoulos and others on the president's staff appeared to tell him of cabinet officers and others of high rank there for urgent, scheduled business, cooling their heels in the outer office. The president waved them away. What he wanted was more, more, more anecdotes about JFK.

27. R. W. Apple, Jr., "Bringing Another Presidency and Inquiry to Mind," *New York Times,* March 8, 1994, p. A13.

28. Jay Rosen, "Who Won the Week? The Political Press and the Evacuation of Meaning," *Tikkun,* July 1993, p. 7.

29. Sidney Blumenthal, "The Anointed: Bill Clinton, Party Favorite," *New Republic,* February 3, 1992, pp. 24–27; Sidney Blumenthal, "The Syndicated Presidency," *New Yorker,* April 5, 1993, pp. 42–47. Blumenthal also wrote a play called *This Town,* produced in Washington and Santa Monica and on radio in 1995, satirizing, as he put it, "the insularity of Washington, its claustrophobia, and the world of a certain segment of the national press corps." Jan Breslauer, "Doing D.C. to Death," *Los Angeles Times,* November 19, 1995, Calendar section, p. 7.

30. Felicity Barringer, "Study Finds More Views Than Facts," *New York Times,* February 19, 1998; Steven Brill, "Pressgate," *Brill's Content,* August 1998, pp. 123–51.

31. James Benet and Janet Elder, "Despite Intern, President Stays in Good Graces," *New York Times,* February 24, 1998, p. A1.

Chapter 6: Private Lives

1. See especially David Broder, *The Party's Over: The Failure of Politics in America* (Harper & Row, New York, 1972), and Dionne, *Why Americans Hate Politics.*

2. Seib, "Many Americans View Washington as a Mess."

3. Seelye, "Voters Disgusted with Politicians."

4. See the series by Donald L. Bartlett and James B. Steele, "America: What Went Wrong?" *Philadelphia Inquirer,* October 20–28, 1991, p. A1, and a series by Bartlett and Steele, "America: Who Stole the Dream?" *Philadelphia Inquirer,* September 8–22, 1996, p. A1.

5. Chris Black, "Tsongas Tells of His Illness and His Plans to Cope," *Boston Globe,* January 15, 1984, p. 1.

6. Erving Goffman, *The Presentation of Self in Everyday Life* (Doubleday-Anchor edition, New York, 1959), p. 12.

7. Joseph Lelyveld's remarks were delivered in a commencement address at the University of Maine, published as "Journalism in the Age of Clinton,"

Downeast Coastal Press, May 12, 1998, p. 21; Sam Howe Verhovek, "Angry Voters Aren't Sure Where to Place the Blame," *New York Times,* October 11, 1998, p. A1.

8. Russell Baker, *The Good Times* (William Morrow, New York, 1989), pp. 335–36; Murray Kempton, "Undertaking Roy Cohn," collected in *Rebellions, Perversities, and Main Events* (Times Books, New York, 1994), p. 261.

9. *Time,* March 2, 1992, p. 16. See also Patterson, *Out of Order,* pp. 64–65.

10. William Empson, *Seven Types of Ambiguity* (New Directions, London, 1947 edition), p. 193.

11. Sissela Bok, *Secrets: On the Ethics of Concealment and Revelation* (Vintage Books, New York, 1989), p. 14.

12. Quoted in Richard F. Hixson, *Privacy in a Public Society* (Oxford University Press, New York, 1987), p. 184.

13. I've drawn here on a thoughtful, provocative thesis developed by Barbie Zelizer in her essay "On Communicative Practice: The 'Other Worlds' of Journalism and Shamanism," *Southern Folklore,* no. 49 (1992), pp. 19–36.

14. Bok, *Secrets,* pp. 254–58.

15. Roosevelt's "brains trust" was celebrated, but so was his distance from and periodic elimination of all in his closest counsel (with the exception of Harry Hopkins, who was at the end more a shadow and instrument than counselor). See Arthur M. Schlesinger, *The Coming of the New Deal* (Houghton Mifflin, Boston, 1958), pp. 522–28; Frank Freidel, *Franklin D. Roosevelt: A Rendezvous With Destiny* (Little, Brown, Boston, 1990), pp. 84–85.

16. Bok, *Secrets,* p. 21.

Chapter 7: Bottom Line

1. Michael R. Beschloss, "Presidents, Television, and Foreign Crises," publication of the Annenberg Washington Program in Communications Policy Studies, Northwestern University, 1993.

2. Taylor Branch, *Parting the Waters: America in the King Years, 1954–1963* (Simon & Schuster, New York, 1988), pp. 112–13, 181–83, 220–25.

3. Seelye, "Voters Disgusted with Politicians"; Seib, "Many Americans View Washington as a Mess."

4. The wave of newspaper merger and acquisition that took on momentum in 1985 was covered astutely by Alex S. Jones, then media reporter for *The New York Times.* See especially Jones's stories "Newspaper Sale: A Trend Continues," February 2, 1985, p. 7, "And Now, the Media Mega-Merger," March 24, 1985, Business section, p. 1, "Gannett Gets Louisville

Papers for 300 Million," May 20, 1986, p. A1, "Sun Newspapers of Baltimore Will be Sold to Times Mirror," May 29, 1986, p. A1, and "The Takeover Threat at Family Newspapers," June 24, 1986, p. D1.

For *The New York Times*'s own long-term corporate course, see coverage of its 1993 purchase of *The Boston Globe,* for example William Glaberson, "Times Co. Acquiring Boston Globe for $1.1 Billion," *New York Times,* June 11, 1993, p. A1, and "Common Traditions Linked Visions for Two Papers," *New York Times,* June 12, 1993, Business section, p. 1; Steve Lohr, "Times Co.'s Strategy: Dominate Northeast," *New York Times,* June 12, 1993, p. 29; Tom Mashberg, "The Modest Mogul," *Boston Sunday Globe,* June 13, 1993, p. 87; Patrick M. Reilly and Gary Putka, "Times-Globe Deal Looks Good—on Paper," *Wall Street Journal,* June 14, 1993, p. B1.

For a contemporary report on the course followed over time by *The Washington Post,* see Iver Peterson, "Think Globally, Focus Locally," *New York Times,* January 12, 1998, p. D1.

5. James Squires, *Read All About It!* (University of Chicago Press, Chicago, 1993), pp. 24–25, 95; Doug Underwood, *When MBAs Rule the Newsroom* (Columbia University Press, New York, 1995), pp. 23, 79.

6. While newspaper industry retail advertising revenue fell from 30.3 percent in 1985 to 22.4 percent in 1997, and circulation revenue from 25.1 percent to 22 percent, classified advertising revenue (with profit margins twice those of retail advertising) *increased* in the same period from 27.4 percent to 35.7 percent. Susan Decker, "Newspaper Cash Margins: Past, Present, and Future," Donaldson, Lufkin & Jenrette report, January 27, 1998. See also "Business Outlook," *Presstime,* September 1997, pp. 30–34.

7. Graham, *Personal History,* pp. 444–54; Evan Thomas, *The Man to See: Edward Bennett Williams* (Simon & Schuster, New York, 1991), pp. 264–66, 268.

8. Squires, *Read All About It!* p. 95; Roberts is quoted in Jonathan Kwitny, "The High Cost of High Profits," *Washington Journalism Review,* June 1990, p. 19.

9. John Morton, "Newspaper Recession Threatens Profits," *Washington Journalism Review,* June 1990, p. 50; Leo Bogart, "The Preprint Predicament," *Presstime,* September 1997, p. 42.

10. David Shaw, "Credibility Vs. Sensitivity: High, Thick Wall Divides Editors and Advertisers," *Los Angeles Times,* February 16, 1987, p. 1; Barbara Gyles, "Ringing Up Retail," *Presstime,* August 1992, p. 14; Bogart, "The Preprint Predicament"; James Lessersohn, vice president of corporate planning, New York Times Company, interview by author, October 22, 1997; Alice Z. Cuneo, "Preprints Extend Reach Throughout the Selling Year," *Advertising Age,* April 20, 1998, p. S14.

11. Joseph Turow, *Breaking Up America: Advertisers and the New Media World* (University of Chicago Press, Chicago, 1997), p. 40.

12. Turow, *Breaking Up America,* pp. 40–42, 54; Gyles, "Ringing Up Retail," p. 14.

13. John Morton, "Direct Mail: The Real Threat to Newspapers," *American Journalism Review,* November 1996.

As I write this in a small town in northern Connecticut where I spend weekends, I'm looking at—diverting from its usual direct route to the trash—such a preprint, delivered regularly by the local post office for *The Hartford Courant,* to which I don't subscribe, consisting of color ads hawking bargains from cut-rate food, tire, and other chain stores, plus two pages of classified ads from the *Courant.*

14. Turow, *Breaking Up America,* p. 129; "Retailing: Who Will Survive?" *Business Week,* November 26, 1990, p. 134; Lessersohn interview, October 22, 1997.

15. Figures on estimated annual U.S. advertising expenditures supplied by the Newspaper Association of America and McCann-Erickson Worldwide.

16. Squires, *Read All About It!* pp. 65, 79, 83.

17. J. Anthony Lukas, *Common Ground* (Vintage Books, New York, 1985), p. 477.

18. Turow, *Breaking Up America,* pp. 44–47.

19. Ibid., pp. 91–93, 137.

Chapter 8: Managing

1. Squires, *Read All About It!* pp. 78–85; Gene Roberts, "Conglomerates and Newspapers," in *Conglomerates and the Media,* Patricia Aufderheide et al. (New Press, New York, 1997), pp. 61, 66–67; Kwitny, "The High Cost of High Profits," p. 19.

2. A compelling added circumstance at *The Boston Globe* was the 1996 expiration date of hundred-year family trusts establishing ownership of the paper.

3. Alex S. Jones, "Knight-Ridder Tries to Balance Profits and News," *New York Times,* August 7, 1989, p. D1; Kwitny, "The High Cost of High Profits," p. 22.

4. Squires, *Read All About It!* pp. 81–82.

5. Alex S. Jones, "For Chicago Tribune Editor, the Power Struggle Ends," *New York Times,* December 11, 1989, p. 37; Kwitny, "The High Cost of High Profits," pp. 19–29.

When I left the editorship of *The Boston Globe* in March 1986, I had served in that role for only fifteen months. Coming to the paper eight years earlier from a predominantly magazine background, I was an "outsider," a controversial choice for the job. The word on my departure was resonant with newsroom politics: always terrific copy.

In fact, my departure came in the midst of two sequences that deeply disturbed the paper's publisher, the principal member of the owning family, the Taylors. First was the purchase by newspaper conglomerates, one by one and gaining momentum after 1984, of family-controlled newspapers across the country. Second was marquee investor Warren Buffett's decision, unrelated to events at the *Globe,* to sell his sizable stake in the paper's parent company stock. The publisher confided in me his shock about these events — and fear (ultimately justified) that their portent was of his own loss of control of the *Globe.* The still-simmering controversy about my appointment, which had bypassed and offended longtime insider aspirants to the job, added to his distress but was by no means the whole of it.

But when backstage maneuvers at the *Globe* threw the publisher into a state of panic about the accumulation of instability at his door, he asked me to switch jobs with my deputy, a safe and known quantity internally, or leave myself. I left.

The ensuing national as well as local news stories focused entirely on me: I was "aloof," I practiced a "management style" alien to the ingrained culture of the *Globe,* and so forth. True, but hardly the whole truth; had it been, my appointment in the first place would have been impossible instead of unusual. An irony that emerged only over time was that had my leave-taking occurred closer to the sequence of industry dislocation that saw the departures of Kovach, Squires, and Roberts from their papers there would have been some press interest, rather than none at all, in the corporate elements of the *Globe* drama.

Accounts of all this are found in Andrew Radolf, "Unrest Resolved at *The Boston Globe,*" *Editor & Publisher,* March 29, 1986, pp. 9–10; James Kelly, "A Matter of Newsroom Style," *Time,* March 31, 1986, p. 59; Alex S. Jones, "Chief Editor Quits at Boston Globe," *New York Times,* March 20, 1986, p. 19; John Strahinich, "The Tinkering Taylors," *Boston Magazine,* September 1992, p. 108; Douglas M. Bailey, "Investor Sells Stake in Globe's Parent," *Boston Globe,* April 16, 1986, p. 73.

6. Alex S. Jones, "Rethinking Newspapers," *New York Times,* January 6, 1991, section 3, p. 1; "Pages and Pages of Pain," *Newsweek,* May 27, 1991, pp. 39–41; Alex S. Jones, "Amid Dark Clouds of Gloom, Newspapers See Some Hope," *New York Times,* December 30, 1991, p. D6.

7. Quoted in Kwitny, "The High Cost of High Profits," p. 22.

8. Sig Gissler, "What Happens When Gannett Takes Over," *Columbia Journalism Review,* November–December 1997, p. 42; Squires, *Read All About It!* pp. 89–91.

9. William Glaberson, "Publishers Look Hard at Content of Papers," *New York Times,* April 27, 1994, p. D17.

10. Jones, "Rethinking Newspapers"; "Pages and Pages of Pain," *Newsweek,* May 27, 1991, pp. 39–41; Jones, "Amid Dark Clouds of Gloom."

11. John Morton, interview by author, October 16, 1998.

12. Patrick M. Reilly, "Knight-Ridder Makes a Costly New Effort to Engage Its Readers," *Wall Street Journal*, December 6, 1990, p. A1.

13. William Glaberson, "Business Outsider Is Moving in at Times Mirror," *New York Times*, May 3, 1995, p. D1; Richard Zoglin, "The News Wars," *Time*, October 21, 1996, p. 68.

14. Iver Peterson, "At Times Mirror, What's the Plan?" *New York Times*, June 26, 1996, p. D1.

15. Neil Hickey, "Money Lust," *Columbia Journalism Review*, July–August 1998, p. 32.

16. Confidential interviews with reporters, critics, and editors at *Time* and *Newsweek*.

17. Howard Kurtz, "*Time* Waits for One Man," *Washington Post*, January 3, 1991, p. B1; Robin Pogrebin, "Foreign Coverage Less Prominent in News Magazines, *New York Times*, September 23, 1996, p. D2; Hickey, "Money Lust," p. 32; Walter Isaacson, "Tailwind: An Apology," *Time*, July 13, 1998, p. 6; Brill, "Pressgate," pp. 133–34; "Don't Call It Journalism," *New York Times*, July 14, 1998, p. A14.

18. Lawrie Mifflin, "Big Three Networks Forced to Revise News-Gathering Methods," *New York Times*, October 12, 1998, p. C1; Bill Carter, "As Their Dominance Erodes, Networks Plan Big Changes," *New York Times*, May 11, 1998, p. 1; Geraldine Fabrikant, "Few Bidders for Networks Despite Good Curb Appeal," *New York Times*, August 31, 1998, p. D6.

19. Ken Auletta, *The Highwaymen: Warriors of the Information Superhighway* (Random House, New York, 1997), pp. xiii, 28, 42.

20. Auletta, *The Highwaymen*, pp. xvi–xvii; "Remember Steam Cars and Plastic Teeth?" *Economist*, September 13, 1986, p. 71; Ralph T. King, Jr., "No, Thanks: The History of Home Technology Is Littered with Flops," *Wall Street Journal*, June 19, 1995, p. R16; David Raymond, "Famous Flops," *Forbes*, June 2, 1997, p. 101; Susan Paterno, "Whither Knight-Ridder?" *Columbia Journalism Review*, January–February 1996, p. 22.

21. William Glaberson, "Newspapers Race for Outlets in Electronic Marketplace," *New York Times*, January 17, 1994, p. C1; Keith J. Kelly, "Times Mirror Shifts Course," *Advertising Age*, June 5, 1995, p. 38.

22. George Bush interview in Munich, Germany, Federal News Service, July 8, 1992; Bill Clinton remarks, U.S. Newswire, May 24, 1993.

23. Beschloss, "Presidents, Television, and Foreign Crises."

24. Lessersohn interview, October 22, 1997.

Jim Squires, once of the Tribune Company, took the contradiction a step further. "Because advertisers want only high-income, well educated readers," he wrote, newspaper publishers, whatever they say to the contrary, "don't really want higher penetration in their market. They want what

magazine publishers have always wanted — higher penetration in the top
35% of the market." Squires, *Read All About It!* p. 89.

Chapter 9: *Trying Something*

1. Sally Deneen, "Doing the Boca," *Columbia Journalism Review*, May–
June 1991, p. 15; Patrick M. Reilly, "Knight-Ridder Makes a Costly New
Effort to Engage Its Readers," *Wall Street Journal*, December 6, 1990, p. A1;
"A Swap of Six Publications," *New York Times*, October 31, 1997, p. D2.

2. Janni Benson, "Three New Ventures," *Quill*, September 1992, pp. 16–
17.

3. William Glaberson, "At the Orange County Register, Journalism for
the Age of the Mall," *New York Times*, January 10, 1994, p. C6; David
Villano, "Has Knight-Ridder's Flagship Gone Adrift? Trouble at *The Miami
Herald*," *Columbia Journalism Review*, January–February 1996, p. 31.

4. "Keys to Our Survival," a Joint Project of the ASNE 1990–91 Readership and Research and 1991 Future of Newspapers Committees, American
Society of Newspaper Editors Foundation, pp. 3–4, 28.

5. Iver Peterson, "Rethinking the News," *New York Times*, May 19,
1997, p. C1.

6. Howard Kurtz, "Diverse View of the News: L.A. Times Minority Staff
Opens Debate on Coverage," *Washington Post*, March 2, 1993, p. E1;
William McGowan, "The Other Side of the Rainbow," *Columbia Journal-
ism Review*, November–December 1993, p. 53; Howard Kurtz, "The Cul-
ture Clash Between the Lines: Minorities in Media Ponder the Price of
Success," *Washington Post*, July 28, 1994, p. C1; Robert Sam Anson, "The
Best of Times, The Worst of Times," *Esquire*, March 1993, pp. 187–88.

7. Edsall and Edsall, *Chain Reaction*, p. 281; "The Simpson Case: Black
and White Justice," *San Francisco Chronicle*, October 4, 1995, p. A18;
Roger Rosenblatt, "A Nation of Pained Hearts," *Time*, October 16, 1996, p.
40; Patricia Cohen, "One Angry Man: Paul Butler Wants Black Jurors to Put
Loyalty to Race Above Loyalty to the Law," *Washington Post*, May 30,
1997, p. B1; Dori Maynard, "Racial Divide Deepened by Class, Gender,
Generation, and Geography," *Seattle Times*, January 18, 1998, p. B5;
Neil A. Lewis, "Black Scholars View Society with Prism of Race," *New York
Times*, May 5, 1997, p. B9.

8. For a disarming account of the infotainment trend in television news,
see Fred Graham, *Confessions of a News Anchor* (Norton, New York,
1990).

9. Walter Goodman, "From Luxury Good to Expensive Wrapper," *New
York Times*, October 21, 1998, p. E7; Bill Carter, "ABC News Divided on
Simulated Events," *New York Times*, July 27, 1989, p. C20; Bill Carter,

"Chicago News Anchor Quits After Station Hires Jerry Springer," *New York Times,* May 4, 1997, p. A1; Steve Johnson, "WMAQ Lesson: Chicago Takes News Seriously," *Chicago Tribune,* May 18, 1997.

10. Auletta, *The Highwaymen,* p. xvii; Lawrie Mifflin, "Should Networks Use Their Newsmagazines to Promote Their Entertainment Shows?" *New York Times,* September 4, 1995, p. A39; Frank Rich, "Media Amok," *New York Times,* May 18, 1996, p. A19; Frank Rich, "The Rodent Rules," *New York Times,* May 6, 1998, p. A23; David Lieberman, "Conglomerates, News, and Children," in *Conglomerates and the Media,* Patricia Aufderheide et al. (New Press, New York, 1997), pp. 142–45; "Size Does Matter," *Economist,* May 23, 1998, p. 57.

11. Lawrie Mifflin, "An ABC News Reporter Tests the Boundaries of Investigating Disney and Finds Them," *New York Times,* October 19, 1998, p. C8; Caryn James, "Here Now the (Wink, Wink) News," *New York Times,* August 27, 1998, p. E5.

12. William Glaberson, "Newspapers Redefining Themselves," *New York Times,* April 26, 1993, p. C1; David Shaw, "Inventing the 'Paper' of Future," *Los Angeles Times,* June 2, 1991, p. A1; Glaberson, "Newspapers Race for Outlets in Electronic Marketplace"; Ken Auletta, "Synergy City," *American Journalism Review,* May 1988, p. 18.

13. Turow, *Breaking Up America,* p. 43.

14. William Glaberson, "Newsprint Costs Trouble Newspapers," *New York Times,* February 6, 1995, p. C1; John Morton, "A Shadow Over the Newspaper Business," *American Journalism Review,* March 1995, p. 56; John Morton, "Are Bean Counters Taking Over?" *American Journalism Review,* April 1995, p. 60.

15. James Sterngold, "A Growing Clash of Visions at the Los Angeles Times," *New York Times,* October 13, 1997, p. D1; Alicia C. Shepard, "Blowing Up the Wall," *American Journalism Review,* December 1997, p. 18; Iver Peterson, "At Los Angeles Times, a Debate on News-Ad Interaction," *New York Times,* November 17, 1997, p. D1; Vernon Bryant, "Why Willes Shakes Up the Status Quo," *Presstime,* May 1998, p. 29.

16. Mark Fitzgerald, "A Crossroads of Strategic Options," *Editor & Publisher,* May 11, 1991, pp. 18–19; Deborah Walker and Jane Wilson, "The Battle for Waterloo," *Presstime,* September 1991.

17. Figures from Audit Bureau of Circulation.

18. James Lessersohn, vice president of corporate planning, New York Times Company, interview by author, February 1, 1998; "Letter from Peter R. Kann, Publisher," *Wall Street Journal,* January 12, 1998, p. A21.

19. Squires, *Read All About It!* pp. 89–90.

20. Sterngold, "A Growing Clash of Visions"; Shepard, "Blowing Up the Wall," p. 18.

21. Peterson, "At Times Mirror, What's The Plan?"

22. Sterngold, "A Growing Clash of Visions"; Shepard, "Blowing Up the Wall," p. 18; Peterson, "At Los Angeles Times, a Debate on News-Ad Interaction."

23. John Morton, "Mark Willes, Again!" *Newspaper Newsletter,* May 31, 1998; John Morton, interview by author, October 16, 1998.

24. Bryant, "Why Willes Shakes Up the Status Quo," p. 28; Sterngold, "A Growing Clash of Visions."

25. Iver Peterson, "The Bottom-Line Publisher of the Los Angeles Times Faces the Hard-Line Skeptics," *New York Times,* March 9, 1998, p. D7; Lisa Bannon, "The Publisher Plans New-Type Faces for the L.A. Times," *Wall Street Journal,* May 18, 1998, p. A1; Felicity Barringer, "Times Mirror Weighs a By-the-Numbers Approach to Expanding Coverage of Minorities," *New York Times,* May 18, 1998, p. D6; Felicity Barringer, "Publisher of Los Angeles Times Apologizes for Gaffe on Women," *New York Times,* June 3, 1998, p. A16.

26. Shepard, "Blowing Up the Wall," p. 18.

27. Peterson, "At Times Mirror, What's The Plan?"; Shepard, "Blowing Up the Wall," p. 18.

28. Felicity Barringer, "The Difficulty in Being Earnest: Efforts to Reinvent The Los Angeles Times Falter," *New York Times,* May 7, 1999, p. C1; Felicity Barringer, "Willes Resigns as Publisher of The Los Angeles Times," *New York Times,* June 4, 1999, p. C6; "The Challenge of Growth: A Journalistic View" (Times Mirror Annual Report, 1998), p. 9.

Chapter 10: Hamilton and Jefferson

1. Susan Paterno, "Whither Knight-Ridder?" *American Journalism Review,* January–February 1996, p. 19.

2. Jay Rosen, "A Scholar's Perspective," in Davis (Buzz) Merritt and Jay Rosen, "Imagining Public Journalism," Roy W. Howard Public Lecture in Journalism and Mass Communications Research, Indiana University, April 13, 1995, p. 21.

3. James Fallows, *Breaking the News: How the Media Undermine American Democracy* (Pantheon, New York, 1996), p. 267.

4. Jonathan Cohn, "Should Journalists Do Community Service?" *American Prospect,* summer 1995, p. 14; Max Frankel, "Fix-It Journalism," *New York Times Magazine,* May 21, 1995, p. 28; Paterno, "Whither Knight-Ridder?" pp. 22–23.

5. Gene Roberts made these remarks in early 1996 in a talk to Freedom Forum Media Studies Center fellows, of whom I was one that year. In his essay "Conglomerates and Newspapers" he condemned "fad-ism and gim-

mickry rampant in today's journalism" and included on his list of manifesta-
tions of that, "sponsoring public meetings on public issues, rather than
covering these same issues in depth" (p. 66).

6. Jay Rosen, "Who Won the Week? The Political Press and the Evacuation of Meaning," *Tikkun,* July 1993, p. 7.

7. Fallows, *Breaking the News,* p. 65.

8. Michael Schudson finds something like my comparison of civic journalism to the Mugwumps in "The Public Journalism Movement and Its Problems," in *The Politics of News/The News of Politics,* ed. Doris Graber,
Denis McQuail, and Pippa Norris (Congressional Quarterly Press, Washington D.C., 1998), p. 140.

Rosen, "A Scholar's Perspective," p. 15; Jay Rosen, "What Should We Be
Doing," *IRE Journal* (Investigative Reporters and Editors), November–
December 1995, p. 7.

9. I'm indebted to James Lessersohn for the Jefferson-Hamilton analogy.

10. Paul Weaver, "Is Television News Biased?" *Public Interest,* winter
1972, p. 69; Patterson, *Out of Order,* pp. 57–60, 68–69, 93.

11. Patterson, *Out of Order,* pp. 30–33, 159.

12. Mike Allen, "Kennelly's Star-Crossed Campaign Spurs Search for
Reasons," *New York Times,* October 3, 1998, p. B1; Sack, "From Sea to
Shining Sea."

Chapter 11: Therefore . . .

1. John Morton, "Hanging Tough When Profits Drop," *American Journalism Review,* October 1998, p. 88.

2. The *Philadelphia Inquirer* series by Donald L. Bartlett and James B.
Steele titled "America: What Went Wrong" ran in October 1991, after
Roberts's departure from the paper's executive editorship, but its assign-
ment was owing to him. Roberts was responsible for *The New York Times*
series "The Downsizing of America," reported and written by a team of
reporters, which ran for a week beginning March 3, 1996.

3. John Morton, interview by author, October 16, 1998.

4. Seymour Topping, administrator, Pulitzer Prizes in Journalism, interview by author, September 30, 1998.

5. William Glaberson, "Survey Finds Newsrooms Discontented," *New
York Times,* November 23, 1992, p. D6; Paul S. Voakes, "Attitudes," *The
Newspaper Journalists of the '90s,* Survey Report of the American Society of
Newspaper Editors, April 1997, pp. 8–17.

6. Jack Fuller, *News Values: Ideas for an Information Age* (University of
Chicago Press, Chicago, 1996), pp. 208–10.

7. Bruce Ackerman, *We the People: Transformations* (Harvard University
Press, Cambridge, 1998), p. 70.

8. Ibid., p. 414.

9. Melissa Healy, "New Movement Plots More Civil Way of Living," *Los Angeles Times*, December 15, 1996, p. A1; Michael D'Antonio and Michael Krasny, "I or We?" *Mother Jones*, May 1994; Lazare, *The Frozen Republic*, p. 3.

10. Mitch McConnell, "The Press as Power Broker," *New York Times*, June 18, 1994, p. A21; Leslie Wayne, "After the Election: Campaign Finance," *New York Times*, November 10, 1996, p. A30; Jeffrey Rosen, "Passing the Buckley," *New Republic*, October 27, 1997, p. 4; "Should Buckley Be Overturned?" (exchange), *American Prospect*, March–April 1998, p. 78; Eric Foner, *The Story of American Freedom* (Norton, New York, 1998), pp. 122–23.

Acknowledgments

This book took form during a sabbatical semester I spent while serving as dean of the Medill School of Journalism at Northwestern University in the winter and spring of 1996. I owe special thanks to Arnold Weber and David Cohen, respectively president and provost of Northwestern at the time the sabbatical was agreed to, for their encouragement in granting what was at Northwestern an unusual form of leave. To Weber, as idiosyncratically skeptical of journalism as he was encouraging of discerning, spirited, collegial exchange about contentious topics, I owe a particular debt for welcoming me as a profession-switcher to the university. The challenge and reward of working with him acted as a stimulus in getting started on this book.

The Freedom Forum Media Studies Center, then at Columbia University under the nurturing leadership of Everette Dennis, granted me a senior fellowship for my sabbatical months in 1996. I thank Dennis and his colleagues for their support as I began the research and drafting of the manuscript.

I'm profoundly grateful to these colleagues, friends, and relatives for their comments on drafts or portions of the manuscript, early on and along the way: Sidney Blumenthal, Alan Brinkley, Richard Ford, Sam Janeway, Alex Jones, James Lessersohn, Nicholas Maltby, Daisy Janeway, Samuel Popkin, Michael Schudson, Richard Todd, Daniel Yergin.

Jonathan Brent is a remarkable editor and friend, hard-nosed and enthusiastic, a scholar and entrepreneur. To him and his colleagues Sally Anne Brown, Susan Donnelly, Lara Heimert, Philip King, Alison Pratt, Nicholas Raposo, and Tina Weiner, my thanks.

Four recent graduates of the Columbia Graduate School of Journalism provided able research assistance from 1996 to 1999. They were, in sequence, Anna Gorman, Matthew Surman, Jennifer Chen, and Nicholas Stein. Working with them had the added value of lifting my hopes for the future of journalism.

A writer's selfish preoccupation can be a cruel and haunting presence in a home. Barbara Maltby put up with that uninvited third party, and came to understand it — and to understand at least a little, I hope, how fine an editor she is. For this and much more I owe her much more than I can say.

A book this steeped in a personal angle of vision does focus the mind at its end by hanging undeniably around one's own neck, and one's own neck alone.

Index